DARWIN
MOVI

S

NG

*Taylor Lambert*

Darwin's Moving
Taylor Lambert
Copyright © Taylor Lambert 2017

Library and Archives Canada Cataloguing in Publication

Lambert, Taylor, 1985-, author
        Darwin's moving / Taylor Lambert.

Includes bibliographical references and index.
Issued in print and electronic formats.
ISBN 978-1-988732-03-9 (softcover).--ISBN 978-1-988732-04-6 (EPUB).--
ISBN 978-1-988732-05-3 (Kindle)

        1. Storage and moving trade--Alberta--Calgary.  2. Calgary (Alta.)--
Social conditions--21st century.  3. Calgary (Alta.)--Economic conditions--
21st century.  I. Title.  II. Title: Moving.

HF5489.C33L36 2017        388'.04409712338        C2017-901283-5
                                                   C2017-901284-3

Editor for the Press: Leslie Vermeer
Cover and interior design: David A Gee
Cover images: RistoArnaudov/iStock
Author photo: Aaron Sostar

NeWest Press acknowledges the support of the Canada Council for the Arts, the Alberta
Foundation for the Arts, and the Edmonton Arts Council for support of our publishing
program. We acknowledge the financial support of the Government of Canada through
the Canada Book Fund for our publishing activities.

NeWest Press
#201, 8540-109 Street
Edmonton, Alberta T6G 1E6
www.newestpress.com

*No bison were harmed in the making of this book.*
Printed and bound in Canada
1 2 3 4 5  19 18 17

A hand that's dirty with honest labour is fit to shake with any neighbour.
—Proverb

# Contents

# Author's Note

I feel compelled to begin by stressing something of considerable importance. To the extent that the stories that follow might cause the reader to wonder just what sorts of people are coming into their home to move their furniture, it must be understood that nothing described is unique to Darwin's Moving as a company. Darwin very generously—and indeed bravely—granted me permission to write an honest account of his business and his employees with the understanding that these tales are reflections of the industry as a whole. I hope the reader will take care to interpret them this way.

My intention is in no way to make Darwin's Moving seem like some shady operation with questionable characters. Every single moving company in your city has people just like this working for them. Some of them are good movers; some of them are lousy movers. The key thing that makes Darwin's Moving one of the best is Darwin himself and the high standards he holds his workers to. Ask around Calgary or Regina and you'll find no shortage of highly satisfied customers.

On to other matters. I have done my best to corroborate and verify the stories told to me in researching this book, but this was not always possible: juvenile criminal records, for example, are sealed. The accuracy of events and claims detailed in these pages is not beyond question. Tall tales abound. Exaggerations and lapses of memory are inevitable. I mention this not to absolve the journalist but to caution the reader.

I have known the three principal subjects of this narrative—Darwin, Jesse and Keith, whom you'll meet in a moment—for many years. I consider all of them to be friends. Despite this, it was only in the course of researching this book that I became familiar with their life stories in both a broad and an intimate sense. I'd known, for example, that Keith had suffered abuse and had a long history of crime and drug addiction. But hours of interviews and probing questions revealed the man and his complexities in a way that years of simply working together did not allow, and the same applies to Jesse and Darwin.

Journalists are generally advised that writing about close acquaintances is full of pitfalls, but there are benefits as well. During those many hours of recorded talks, each man was forthcoming in a way he never would have been with a stranger. I heard the bragging, laughing stories they tell to anyone with ears, of course. But the emotional, difficult, shadowed parts of their lives that, in many ways, they have not fully grappled with themselves—these are the parts of a person shared only with those who have earned a great deal of trust.

And so while I caution the reader that I have not been able to fact check every claim, I will also state that I have personal faith in the broad if not exact truth of these accounts, enough so to publish them with my name attached. Dates may be off, details may be fuzzy or exaggerated at times, but outright fabrication seems to me an exceptionally unlikely possibility. Both Jesse and Keith understood their real names would not be in the book, and I doubt they would lie for glory under this cloak of anonymity. Moreover, I corroborated enough of their tales for them to earn my trust. I leave it to the reader to determine what this endorsement is worth.

On to the debts of gratitude. I could spend many words expressing appreciation to the people who made this book possible, but I would still come up short. So, for the sake of brevity, my sincere thanks to Jesse, Keith, Barb and the others who shared their personal stories; and especially to Darwin, not only for being crazy enough to let me write this book, but for ten years of friendship. Thanks as well to Brian Gabrial, who convinced me that a book about furniture movers was not, in fact, a terrible idea; to Leslie Vermeer, whose editing made this book better; and to NeWest Press, whose support brought this book into your hands.

Finally, with the exception of Darwin and his family, all names have been changed to protect both the guilty and the innocent.

# A Day In The Life

As I round the corner of the buildings that ring the gravel truck yard, I see three figures at a distance near Darwin's pickup truck. Darwin and Keith are easily recognizable even from afar. The third figure, with his back to me and hood up, might be Jesse. He turns, notices me and starts walking to me. It's Jesse. He pulls his hood off. Did Jesse shave his head? The figure nears. That's not Jesse. "How you doin', brother?" Oh my god, it's Ricky Roy.

He shakes my hand and embraces me. "I'm good, man, how you doin'?"

Ricky's voice rises sharply in pitch as he answers with musical bounciness. "Aw, I'm doin' all right, man. Living the dream."

Ricky looks much older than the last time I saw him. His face is worn and wrinkled well beyond his years. "You got some more grey hair," he says in melodic voice as he flicks my hair with one finger.

I laugh. "It's the stress of working for Darwin."

"Yeah, I got some, too," he says, rubbing a hand over his buzzed haircut. "Turning forty soon." I hadn't realized that Ricky was ten years older than me, and I'm struck by the thought that I am now the age he was when we first started working together.

We walk to the pickup next to the warehouse where Keith is smoking. Darwin walks to throw something in the dumpster across the yard before I can say hello.

"How you doin', Keith?" I say.

"Mornin', Ty." He always gets my name wrong. Nothing personal, just a tired brain worn from decades of substance abuse.

"Ready for another beautiful day?"

He inhales the cigarette and answers in his rough gravel voice. "Fuck, my shoulder's fucking acting up again today."

"Aw, muffin."

"Yeah, muffin's complaining again."

Ricky and I continue catching up and he tells me he has cancer.

"What kind?"

"Colon."

"Jesus, Ricky."

"Ah, it's fine. It ain't terminal or nothing. Doesn't stop me from living the dream." He grins and sways in a physical demonstration of his nonchalance. "Hey!" he suddenly barks, his bright eyes tightening as he looks over my shoulder. Ricky marches away from me and I turn to see Jesse grinning. They shake hands and Ricky says something quietly to him with a smile.

Darwin returns from the dumpster and walks into the warehouse. I follow him. "So, Ricky Roy." He looks at me with a moment of confusion and then understands. "Yeah," he laughs, "I was pretty desperate."

The trucks are running and ready to go, tidy and loaded with the necessary equipment and supplies. Darwin hands me the paperwork and says that it's me, Jesse and Keith working together. He's on another move with Ricky. He knows nothing about our job other than it is going from Crestmont to Springbank. Big, small, challenging, straightforward—anything could await us. We never really know.

It's the first time I've seen Jesse since he blew up Nazi Bill. Apparently bored at home one day the previous week, Jesse started burning things other than wood in his backyard fire pit. This escalated to aerosol cans and propane tanks. These he threw into the fire before running indoors and filming the result from a window. Bill unwittingly and unfortunately entered the scene just as the explosion occurred, suffering second-degree burns on his face and hands. Jesse pulls out his phone to show Ricky and I the footage. On the small screen of his flip phone little is discernible except the explosion and someone yelling, "What are you doing?!"

"Hey, Snuggles!" Ricky grins at me as he uses my old nickname. "You said you were going to write about me in one of your books." Jesse jumps in with excitement. "Yeah! You said you were going to write a book about me, too!" I insist I made no such promises; they don't care, it's not the point. We laugh and joke about it until it's time to go.

Jesse declares that he is driving, which is fine by me. Driving is, for Jesse, a way to be in charge, and to avoid the boredom that comes to him so easily. Keith, the smallest of us, sits in the middle of the blue truck's bench seat, trying to keep his legs to the side of the stick shift extending from the floor in front of him.

From the Foothills industrial district we take Glenmore to Sarcee and then the Trans-Canada to Canada Olympic Park, or more precisely the McDonald's across from it, where we stop so Keith and Jesse can get breakfast. I stand outside the truck in the cold morning air looking at the ski jumps until they return with sandwiches and coffees and cigarettes and we get back on the highway for the short drive to Crestmont.

Our customer arrives at the house at the same time we do, which is fortunate because the pit stop has made us half an hour late. Shelley is in her early thirties. She is pleasant but clearly stressed. We introduce ourselves and ask her to give us a walk-through of the house. Just off the entryway is a large aquarium full of water and fish. "You guys take these, right?" asks Shelley.

"We don't normally take them when they're full," says Jesse.

He's being kind. Who on earth would think it sensible to take forty gallons of water and living things enclosed in glass on a moving truck? Shelley looks worried. "I didn't bring anything to put them in," she says. We suggest a bucket, or plastic baggies. For a long moment she looks lost. Then she snaps out of it. "Okay, I'll deal with that," and we continue the tour.

There are no boxes, not a one. Shelley and her husband Dan have already moved everything they could to the new house. All that remains is furniture. The house is two storeys plus a basement, just under three thousand square feet. In the basement there is a sectional, an overstuffed chair, a wood armoire, and a long wooden table with a heavy marble top. On the main floor there is a kitchen table with chairs, couches and bookshelves, a TV stand (but the TV stays), and two buffets. Upstairs are the master bedroom and the rooms of their two young daughters, as well as a large office. Aside from the usual bookcases and desks and beds, there are two items of note. One is a large glass terrarium with two box turtles and an armadillo lizard. The other is an eight-foot by eight-foot glass-and-wood cabinet that is clearly quite expensive and heavy. The backyard contains a wooden deck table and barbecue. In the garage is a treadmill.

We set to work, first laying out the floor runners and affixing moving blankets to the railings. Without boxes the lightest things are kitchen chairs and couch cushions, and these we put in the top kick that hangs over the cab of the truck. Either Jesse or I am normally in charge of packing the truck, but he will do it today as his back is in pain. Keith's shoulder injury is also a problem. I hope to myself that we'll be able to finish the job without injury to either movers or furniture.

Keith and I alternate between carrying out one-man pieces separately and two-man pieces together. Jesse packs into the load what we set down in the truck. Packing is an art, a far more difficult job than it seems. It is a giant Tetris game, filling the truck by arranging boxes and furniture into securely fitting layers that we call tiers—except the pieces are irregularly shaped, they need to be protected from damage, their weight must be taken into account, and they don't disappear when you complete a tier. It takes time to maximize efficient usage of space, but on a big move like today, it's crucial.

That said, Jesse is taking more time than he ought and the truck soon gets jammed up with furniture. He blames us for setting pieces down in the centre and not on the sides, which is valid but not really the point. Keith and I take our time to let Jesse catch up on his backlog.

The load goes well and without incident. Shelley manages to empty the aquarium, and we convince her that it will be safer in her vehicle, though we agree to take the turtle habitat minus its inhabitants. Keith and I carry everything, with the exception of the occasional chair or mirror or other small one-man pieces that Jesse grabs as he packs. Nothing is particularly heavy. But now it's time to tackle the big boy.

Jesse prepares the massive cabinet, wrapping it with two pads and then covering it in plastic shrink wrap to aid our grip. Keith's shoulder is already getting worse and, fearful, I quietly ask Jesse to carry the cabinet with me. He says he can't on account of his back—and Jesse never, ever declines a chance to prove his considerable strength, so he must really be hurting—but I insist he stay with Keith just in case the worst happens and the weight becomes too much. He agrees.

Great weight is one challenge, great size another. Combined in one item, these characteristics have their effects multiplied significantly. Anything eight feet tall, eight feet wide and four feet deep is difficult to manoeuvre. As I tip it toward Keith, I estimate it to be around four hundred pounds. Keith is cradling the top of the tilted piece, and I will lift from the diagonally opposite edge, walking backwards. At this angle the width of the piece becomes its height, and the edge I need to carry is hanging high over the stairwell. Too high, in fact, for me to hold the weight in my hands near waist level, which would be the most comfortable and stable position. Instead I must move down two steps and lift the edge with my arms nearly vertical above me, one step at a time. We do this for three steps, and then we must start to turn. To make the corner, Keith has to tilt the cabinet up vertically without losing his grip, and Jesse helps him as I lift and swing at the same time and we set it down smoothly on the landing having turned ninety degrees. Now we have nine more steps to the bottom.

Keith is finding it difficult to carry the piece without the weight tilted toward him. But to tilt it raises the edge I must lift from, and it's too difficult to keep it steady when I must lift it over my head. The size and weight of the cabinet is proving difficult on the stairs. Keith asks for a strap, and Jesse runs out to get it. The orange forearm strap is too short to loop around the bottom of the behemoth. Jesse runs out again and returns with two white piano straps, which he joins together. Wrapping each end of the strap around his wrists, Keith can now lift the piece with the weight tilted further toward me. With great effort we make it to the bottom, and I use the forearm strap so we can carry the cabinet out nearly on its side to clear the front doorway.

Our greatest trial of the load-up is complete, but two more soon arise: the large vertical freezer in the basement is in fact coming, despite what we were initially told; and the barbecue is chained to the deck and the key is at the new house.

The truck is getting full, and I go outside to estimate our chances with Jesse. For all his skill and experience as a mover, one of Jesse's weaknesses is an overabundance of confidence that often clashes with the principles of finite space. We agree things are looking tight. What about the customer's pickup truck? It has a small bed, but we might be able to get the treadmill and barbecue in there with the tailgate down.

We ask Dan, and he's game to try. Keith and I load the treadmill in, and there appears to be room left for the rather wide barbecue—which brings us to the second problem. Dan asks if we have bolt cutters for the lock, but we do not. (Keith makes a joke about parolees not being allowed to carry them, but fortunately the customers don't hear him.) Dan offers to go get the key, but Jesse suggests trying to break the lock, and Dan agrees. Standing on the grass below the deck, Keith and I hold up a moving blanket between the deck and the hanging lock and chain. Jesse attacks it with a hammer repeatedly, his frustration growing with each failed swing.

Dan watches as Jesse passes twenty swings, then thirty. The lock is battered but closed, holding strong. "Remind me to buy a Masterlock," I quip. Jesse glares angrily at his enemy, no doubt thinking of tearing it apart with his bare hands and teeth. "The problem," he says, "is the pad. It's too soft."

"Do you have any plywood?" I ask Dan, and he does. Keith and I switch the pad for the wood and it still takes Jesse another twenty violent swings before the lock surrenders.

The barbecue fits sideways on the truck, allowing us to close the tailgate and strap the load down. Now we'll get the rest on the moving truck. The freezer and the last few items go on, and then all that's left is the turtle tank and some outside planters. But now it's time for a break: Dan and Shelley have bought us pizza and beer.

The beer is a choice of Coors Light or Bud Light, but it is not unwelcome after nearly four hours of work. The pizza is hot and greasy and delicious. The five of us stand in the kitchen and eat while the turtles try to clamber out of the kitchen sink with little prospect of success.

Shelley make a comment about how they have too much stuff, which prompts Jesse to ask how many pairs of shoes she owns and how many she would take on a three-day vacation. Shelley protests that she is "getting better" and has cut down on her collection, but it's still too many for Dan, apparently. He punches his open palm dramatically and says "The wife beater's coming out tonight," which gets a big laugh from Jesse. "Women love their shoes," says Jesse. "No," says Dan, "anything that costs money, that's women, that's what they love."

The conversation meanders from there, somehow arriving at the recent case of the armoured truck guard who murdered several of his colleagues in a pathetic attempt to steal the money they were securing. Jesse says he heard the guy got five years. This upsets Dan.

"No, you know what? You know what he shoulda got?" Dan says as he gestures with his Bud can for effect. "They should hang guys like that. Yeah. Do it at the Saddledome, I'll come watch. I mean, hey, you pay three hundred to go see the Flames. I'd go watch that."

We stuff ourselves full of pizza and beer and then it's time to finish loading. Even without the treadmill and barbecue on our truck there is just barely enough space for the remainder plus our equipment. As Keith and I lift the ramp to carry it to the side of the truck, Jesse makes a motion and whispers to him: Let's roll a joint. There is a brief discussion of who has rolling papers and then Jesse speaks loudly to Dan while Keith and I put the ramp away.

"So, we're just going to stop at a corner store on the way if that's all right."

"Oh, what do you need to buy?"

"Ah, cigarettes."

"Oh, okay, well, I was going to say you guys could follow me."

"Well, we've got a map, so we should be fine."

"It's not on that map," I tell Jesse, "I checked."

"Oh." Jesse pauses. "You know what, we don't need cigarettes."

"No, I can meet you guys there at the store, and then we can go."

"Nah, it's fine. We'll just follow you."

As we close up the back doors, I tell Jesse I'll drive. He believes this to be an offer, and he shrugs and says okay. But I don't like Jesse driving when he's stoned and distracted. It was a declaration, not an offer, but his fragile ego requires the pretense.

We get into the cab and I follow Dan out of Crestmont back onto the Trans-Canada and we head west out of the city. It's not a long drive, only about fifteen minutes door to door, and the boys have rolled and smoked before we're on the highway. "I didn't really need cigarettes," laughs stoned Jesse, "I just wanted more time to get high."

The house is in Springbank, a huge area just west of Calgary that represents the New Albertan Dream: enormous modern homes set far apart with large open rolling fields and trees and no need for fences. The new and improved suburbia, for those who can afford it, complete with enough space to park your fleet of motorized toys and keep you at shouting distance from your neighbours. Dan and Shelley's house is a tall bungalow perched high above a walk-out basement barely sunk below ground level.

I slowly back the truck up the narrow winding driveway, and we drop the ramp as close to the front door as we can, which isn't close: five stairs leading to a long pathway, and then a dozen or so steep, narrow steps up to the house. This added walk, repeated countless times, will add significant work to our day.

We start unloading. Shelley is not here yet and Dan doesn't know where many of the items go. It's clear now that they do in fact have far too much furniture: though the house is a few hundred square feet larger than the old one, there is already a couch set inside in addition to the two on the truck and we are soon running out of floor space to set things down.

Jesse's back is feeling better and he is happy to help carry furniture. But now we have three men working and most of the items are two-man pieces. Fortunately Dan seems relaxed and unrushed, so it's not a problem if one guy has to wait on the truck for someone to return from the house.

The off-load goes smoothly. Shelley arrives with their daughters, a four-year-old and two-year-old. The older one is friendly and goofy and talks a lot; she takes a shine to Jesse. There is also a dog, a labradoodle who is unusually unafraid of running onto the truck.

It is time for the cabinet, the only truly challenging piece we have. It is destined for the office just off the front entryway. The stairs leading to the front door are shallow and steep, eleven steps to the top. I quietly tell Jesse that he needs to take it with me. I don't trust Keith, whose shoulder is getting weaker and who seems tired today. The job has gone well so far and we'd hate to have our day ruined with the end in sight. Jesse's back is feeling sturdy enough for him to agree.

We strap the padded cabinet to the appliance dolly. We use a ratchet strap because the strap on the dolly is not only too short, but also broken.

"Beat it," Keith tells Jesse as he sees us preparing to carry it.

"You're not needed, old man," I say.

"I'm doin' it witcha."

He protests for awhile that he ought to carry it, but not too much. Jesse and I tip the piece to me. Because the cabinet is far too tall for me to grip the handles of the dolly, I must support the piece from its top edge.

As we go slowly down the ramp, Jesse pushes hard against the cabinet to slow its momentum and we make a soft landing on the driveway. I swing the piece so that I am walking backwards and we go up the five stone steps leading to the walkway. For each of these, Jesse must lift the cabinet enough to slide and roll the dolly up to the next level. Unable to pull from the handles, I can do little to help. But this is nothing compared to what lies ahead.

Past the walkway I turn and walk up the first couple of steps of the main staircase. We push the dolly's wheels up against the front of the first stair, and I assume a wide stance and check my grip.

"Ready?"

"Ready."

"Go!" Jesse grunts and strains his considerable muscles to lift the piece up one step. "Go!" Another step. "Go!" And another, building a rhythm. I keep the cabinet tilted toward me and carry the weight that comes with each lift as I quickly advance backwards in unison with my partner. The dolly's wheels barely fit on the narrow steps and we have to be careful not to let it roll back down between lifts.

We reach the top and find the tilted piece is too tall for the doorway. I squat uncomfortably low and shuffle backwards. We make it inside, only to find that the office archway is slightly lower and I must perform the same contortion once more.

Keith takes it upon himself to begin setting up the beds while Jesse and I continue emptying the truck. This is welcome, not only because it will save his shoulder and because Keith took the beds apart in the first place, but also because most movers despise finicky nuts-and-bolts bits-and-pieces assembly/disassembly work.

Jesse and I alternate between folding some of the many moving blankets strewn about and carrying furniture off. It all has to get done before we stop the clock, and aside from the small respite that folding allows, the dozens of pads lying around the truck pose a tripping hazard when we're carrying something. This is the slowest part of a move, or so it seems. The initial impression of rapid progress has vanished and now it seems to take forever for each tier of the load to disappear. But within a couple of hours the truck is empty, and Jesse goes inside to help Keith rearrange the master bedroom suite while I finish cleaning up the truck. It is dusk by the time Jesse does the bill, which comes to just over two grand.

"Hey, you guys smoke," says Dan as Shelley writes out a cheque. "Do you smoke cigars?" He's already walking toward the house when we all answer affirmatively. Dan returns with a large box of assorted and expensive Cuban cigars for us to pick from. "I don't smoke," says Dan as I grab a Romeo y Julieta Punch in a silver tube.

Come inside for pizza and beer, they say, and I wonder whence it came. Inside, sure enough, are two more pizzas and cold Bud Light waiting for us. We wash our hands with thanks for the generosity and the five of us sit at the table while the girls screech and play noisily. At one point they rush out of the kitchen, and Keith interrupts Dan's story.

"Sorry, I just noticed," he says softly in his gravel voice, "she took the scissors with her." Shelley calls her daughter back, who glumly returns the pilfered cutters.

Once we've stuffed ourselves we say thank-you again and head out in the darkness to our waiting truck. Jesse needs money tonight, so he calls Darwin and asks if we can stop by. It's out of the way and he hasn't asked me, but I don't work in the morning so I don't mind. Keith is going to stop at Jesse's to buy pot and then come to the yard with me to retrieve his bike and cycle home.

On the drive, Keith calls his wife to tell her he's done work, he's coming home with pot, and that he'll ask Darwin for an advance. The topic apparently changes because Keith says "Who? Who? Who?" louder and with more emphasis each time. "No. NO. Well, he'd better not be there when I get home or I'll cut that nigger's throat. No. Okay. Yeah, soon. Okay, put him on." A pause, and then his young son is on the line and Keith's voice jumps an octave.

"Hey buddy, you being good? Yeah? Mom says you're being whiny. Yeah? You be good, okay? You wanna fight when I get home? When I get home I'm going to wake you up and punch you in the nose. You're going to hit me?" He laughs raspingly. "Okay, buddy. I'll be home soon. Love you. Yep. Bye."

The pin in the parking brake handle has fallen out again when we get to Darwin's, so I have to sit in the truck with my foot on the brake pedal while they go borrow advances off the boss. They come running back around the corner—presumably out of consideration for their driver—and we head into the city.

I wait at Jesse's house in Bankview with my foot on the brake and Keith runs back outside after about five minutes, a quick and efficient drug deal. I live three blocks from Jesse but I try not to think of how close I am to home, how late it already is, and how long it will take me to get back here. We meander through Marda Loop and take Crowchild south to Glenmore.

Keith, unprompted, attempts to explain his comments about cutting the throat of the black man his wife mentioned. "So, like, I got a problem with certain drugs. Like crack. And I've been good, I've kept clean and kept that shit out of my life, you know. But then this guy calls, and my wife tells me this guy calls. Like, I'm trying to stay away from that shit and then she's like, 'Oh, your friend TJ called.' Like, what am I supposed to do with that information?"

I nod and murmur in agreement as I turn the truck into the dark yard and shut off the engine. Keith turns on the cab light and starts rolling a joint for my walk to the bus. I rarely indulge anymore, but it's been a long day and it's a long bus ride home, and Keith is more than happy to have a chance to repay me for going out of my way after the job.

"It's like that Marilyn Manson song," I say. "'I Don't Like the Drugs, But the Drugs Like Me.'"

"The drugs fucking love me, man," Keith mutters as he licks the rolling paper to seal it, and I briefly wonder if his hepatitis C is transferable by saliva. "Here you go, buddy."

"Thanks."

We lock the doors and shut off the lights. Keith lights a cigarette and gives me his lighter to take with me. "I don't smoke when I bike anyway." He unlocks his bike and climbs on and we say good night and go our separate ways. I jaywalk across Glenmore as I smoke my joint and get to the bus stop just as the bus arrives. Ninety minutes later, after a train ride and another bus, I am home.

# How I Got Here

Darwin's Moving & Deliveries is a small Calgary company: two trucks and a non-permanent crew, with Darwin Schulz at the head of it all and his wife Barb running the home office. I have worked for Darwin's Moving for nearly a decade, which was never how it was supposed to be. To be sure, I have tried my best to leave. For most of those years, I was a sporadic employee, coming through and departing again, each time certain to be leaving the job behind forever. It's only been during this current "temporary" stint—two years and counting—that I've accepted the perks and perils of furniture moving and my small but reliable role with Darwin's.

In 2006, I was finishing my second year of journalism school at Concordia University in Montreal and looking for a summer job. During the school year I worked at the campus computer store, but there were no hours in the summer and I wanted a gig at a bar or restaurant. I had no relevant experience and rudimentary French, and I eventually gave up and went home to Calgary, which was entering another major boom and desperate for workers.

Despite applying everywhere for lucrative construction jobs, I somehow had no employment by the time June rolled around. I was getting desperate. My friend Dave mentioned that his cousin owned a moving company and was always looking for workers. He gave me Darwin's number. I called, and the voice on the line sounded pleasant and friendly. He told me to come in for my first day on Saturday.

I showed up at the yard, which was then on an Inglewood side street adjacent to a storage facility. At the end of the driveway that led to the property there was a small building that housed the storage company's office, and a gate to the locked units on the right. To the left were stacks of shipping containers and an flat gravel area past an open gate. I looked for a sign that said Darwin's Moving. It was a business, so logically it should have a sign directing people somewhere.

But there was nothing. I walked back to check the address posted at the entrance. This was the place. Darwin noticed me, this skinny, lost, twenty-one-year-old gangle of a young man, and walked across the yard to retrieve me.

Two things immediately struck me when he introduced himself. The first was that he bore a fair facial resemblance to his cousin Dave; the second was that Darwin was a giant of a man, and I was suddenly keenly aware of my lack of visible strength. As we walked towards the trucks in the open gravel area, I worried that I had gotten myself into a job I wouldn't be able to handle.

The gravel yard was ringed with shipping containers, and several moving trucks were parked there. Darwin had two moving trucks, parked at the far end, which I would come to know quite well over the following decade: a blue International with side doors and a box extending over the cab, and a slightly shorter white International with a roll-up door at the back. The blue truck had only his company name on the cab doors, but the white truck was emblazoned with huge letters and an odd lake scene on the sides and rear of the box.

It was just me and Darwin that day. I climbed up into the passenger seat and we headed west through Inglewood. He didn't tell me where we were going.

We talked, trying to find common ground. Darwin had a gentleness in his voice and demeanour that belied his refrigerator-sized stature. He was well spoken and polite, keen to listen. He was my new boss, and therefore I was eager to please and somewhat intimidated, but he was a very likeable man and I soon felt at ease.

We talked about cousin Dave, our only known commonality. We talked about Montreal and journalism. We talked about moving, which he had been doing for more than twenty years and which I was eager to learn, not least because I had family and friends who were doubtful of my capacity to perform manual labour.

As we talked, Darwin steered the great white boat through downtown to Bow Trail and then to Sarcee Trail. Driving south, approaching Signal Hill, he pointed to an old apartment complex near Richmond Road and said that was our destination.

From there, the day's fragments are scattered in my memory. I do recall it was an Asian family we moved and they didn't speak much English. I remember filling the elevator with their cheap and worn furniture. I don't recall where we moved them to. The whole thing was fairly unremarkable. Movers remember specific jobs because of their oddities, things that stick out, things that go wrong, things that are unusually big or heavy or challenging, or memorable customers. That is why I vividly remember the second job we did that day.

It was in the northwest somewhere; Varsity sticks in my mind, though I can't be sure. We'd dropped the moving truck off and arrived in Darwin's pickup for an internal move, from the house to the garage. I think they were renovating or something.

We were to move a dining room set: several chairs around a circular glass tabletop which sat on a base. We moved the chairs first, then prepared to tackle the tabletop. It was massive. It was very heavy, a couple hundred pounds for sure. Darwin and I lifted it off the base and spun it vertical. I was not yet a mover. I didn't have the experience or technique. I didn't have the powerful hand strength or calloused palms to improve my grip. As we walked with this glass hovering two feet above the tile floor, I felt it slipping.

"I can't make it," I said, panicking. Darwin looked at me with some combination of *oh no* and *for fuck's sake*. "Okay," he said calmly, still walking backwards, "let's get to the carpet." There was a small rug at the front door and we hurried to it. The glass slipped from my hand before I could set it down gently, and it landed with a hard thud.

"Easy," Darwin said as I wiped my sweaty hands on my pants. I had never been in a situation like this. Never before had I had a job where my physical performance was all that mattered, where my ability to perform as required was extremely questionable, and failure to perform would mean smashing a huge, expensive piece of glass under the watchful, critical eyes of the customer and my new boss.

I tried to lift, but my grip was tenuous. I felt the curved glass sliding no matter how hard I squeezed my thumb and fingers against it. Darwin's side had a single handprint; mine was a smeared mess of sweat and terror.

Darwin offered me work gloves from his truck. They had no gripping power, but they at least kept my perspiration out of the equation, and I managed to struggle in several stages to the garage. It was profoundly embarrassing. The customer was plainly worried during the whole ordeal. Darwin was patient, but I assumed this would be my first and last day working for him.

Nevertheless, I spent the rest of the summer moving furniture ninety hours a week. I started at fifteen dollars per hour and was at seventeen dollars an hour by the time I left for Montreal ten thousand dollars richer. I came back every summer during university, and usually worked a bit over the Christmas holidays. After graduation I went on to forge my career in journalism, which took many unorthodox turns along the way. I never lived in Calgary during this time, but once in a while I would work a bit for Darwin when I was in town for an extended visit. In 2012, I moved back to the city and shifted my career to freelance and independent journalism. To cover the inevitable gaps between that meagre source of income and Calgary-level living costs, I turned once again to moving furniture.

The crews always changed. My first summer it was Ricky, then Jesse. I didn't work with Keith until more recently. Aside from a few others of note, everyone else just came and went, either to better or lesser things. No one stays. No one lasts.

But they were largely drawn from the same well: working poor, frequently with addiction issues and criminal histories, usually financially unstable and often irresponsible with their personal choices. They came from a class more comfortable in the 'hood of Forest Lawn than the trendiness of Kensington. They spoke with the same oh-yaah accent and drank double-doubles from Tim Hortons and smoked cheap cigarettes and peppered their speech with compulsive cursing and used degrading language when speaking of women or minorities. There are of course real and complex people behind these generalizations. But these commonalities broadly encompass the vast majority of furniture movers I have met over the years, whether they worked for Darwin or another company.

I did not come from this class; neither did Darwin, for that matter. But there is no way to understand class lines without crossing them. There was without a doubt a degree of discomfort, of unease, of uncertainty as I interacted with these men at first. They largely had the same skin colour as me, they spoke the same language, they came from the same country. But we came from different *places*: our homes, our family lives, our friends, how we were raised, the opportunities and obstacles we faced along the way, all of this was starkly different because they grew up poor and I did not. Ultimately, the economics of class were largely responsible for my discomfort, though it took me a while to trace that logic.

My uneasiness would vanish with time and understanding. I learned to see these men as human beings, not stereotypes. I learned their stories, how they got to where they are, and why they struggle to advance. They are the Other Calgary, the flip side of the boom coin, the ones who can't afford sky-high rent or nice cars or trendy restaurants and craft beer. They live separated from those things the middle class loves about the new Calgary. They are people I would never have met under other circumstances. Moving furniture taught me more about humanity, and about my own shortcomings, than I could have ever imagined.

# Darwin

Darwin Werner Schulz was born in October 1968 in Estevan, Saskatchewan. He lived with his parents in the nearby town of Midale until his parents divorced not long after the birth of his sister Lisa. His father, Werner, won custody of the children but they were sent for a while to live with their grandparents in North Portal, on the North Dakota border. Darwin started school during this year of turmoil.

Things soon changed once again as Darwin and Lisa were sent back to their father. Along with Werner's new girlfriend and her son, the family decamped for Westlock, Alberta, eighty-five kilometres north of Edmonton. His father found work as a mechanic for a slaughterhouse, and his job kept him out of the house enough for Darwin to start getting into trouble at a young age.

At first it was small things: lying to teachers, stealing gum or candy from a store. Before age ten, Darwin was breaking and entering homes on his paper route when he knew the residents were away. He did this with friends, stealing whatever petty cash they found lying around, vandalizing the house.

During one break-in, Darwin and his friend Clyde found some .22 calibre rifles and Mason jars of preserves in the basement. Like any good ten-year-old boys, they lined the jars up on a sawhorse and fired at them from the other side of the basement.

One night the troublemaking went too far, a veritable buffet of youthful rampaging. The meal began with a fairly typical B&E hors d'oeuvre at the home of a vacationing family on Darwin's paper route. But this appetizer came with a flambé twist: the boys lit a small fire in the living room to go along with the usual vandalism and petty theft. They moved on to other delectable criminal courses, breaking into the school as well as the public swimming pool, where they busted out some canoes and took them out on the water.

Their thrilling movable feast culminated with a memorable dessert course: Darwin smashed the glass door of a motorcycle shop and they entered to steal a motorcycle, which they pushed all the way to the railway tracks. The boys were too small to lift it over the tracks, so they hid their booty in tall grass nearby and called it a night.

The following day, Darwin bragged to his friend Matthew about the evening's events. He thought nothing of letting his buddy in on the secret, but he would soon come to regret it.

It was Lisa who told Darwin that Matthew had gone to the police with the information. It was a surprising betrayal by a friend he trusted, but Darwin didn't have much time to be shocked. The family whose house they had vandalized returned from vacation, and the father drove over to see Darwin.

*We're back from holiday, so you can start our paper again on Monday.*

*Oh, sure thing.*

*By the way, our house got broken into while we were away. You wouldn't happen to know anything about that, would you?*

*Oh, no. I never saw anything.*

The man's expression and tone darkened. *Well, the police are investigating and they're dusting for fingerprints, so when they find something, you're going to be in shit!*

His situation growing more frightening by the minute, Darwin decided on the most sensible course of action he could think of: blame someone else. He set out on foot for the police station, running so he could tell the cops as soon as he could that it was Matthew who had done all of those things. His route took him by the tracks where he and Clyde had left the motorcycle and saw that the cops were already there inspecting it. He needed a new plan.

Rather than blame Matthew, Darwin decided he now had to confront him. He turned and ran to his friend's house, where he found Matthew had locked himself inside. There were old washing machines along the side of the house and Darwin stood on one of these to speak to Matthew through an open window.

*Tell them you lied, tell them you made it up!* He was begging his friend, terrified of the consequences. *Here, I've got this money we took from houses, you can have it, just tell the cops you lied!*

*Stay out, Darwin!* was the reply, and Matthew pointed a handgun at him. *Get back, stay out!*

Darwin left. The cops busted him and Clyde. They were fingerprinted. Along with a *you'll regret this the rest of your life* lecture, Darwin's father gave him a licking with his belt until his legs were good and bruised.

But there were no further repercussions, at least not legally. He never went to court, never received a sentence, never owed anything to anyone for his actions. What aspects of the situation Darwin the boy might have missed—whether his father paid for the damages, or whether charges were ever seriously pursued—Darwin the adult can only guess at thirty-five years later.

But there was secondary fallout from these events. For some time, restless Darwin had been asking his father if he could go live with his mother in Regina. His mom came to visit them on occasion with her second husband Ed, a successful dentist, and their nice Lincoln and nice clothes. Darwin's father's wage was enough for the family to live on, but they did not have a great deal of money, certainly not for luxuries. But his father always said no whenever Darwin asked to leave. Until now. Now he told his son, *Write her a letter and tell her what you've done here. And if she wants you, you can go.*

He wrote the letter. Yes, his mom said, you can come. Darwin moved in with her, Ed and their daughter Deirdre in time to start grade six at A.E. Perry School in Regina.

Ed may not have been thrilled about his wife's rambunctious budding criminal moving in, but he certainly did his best to take care of Darwin. Ed would drive him to his hockey games when he was able to. Darwin can't recall his mother ever going to a game. The family went on vacation together in California and Las Vegas, staying in nice hotels. Darwin's father couldn't afford trips like that. The only previous time Darwin had stayed in a hotel before was on a trip to Lethbridge. He fell in love with this new life of nice things and relative comfort.

But he was still getting into trouble: the break-and-enters had been replaced with fights at school and bullying, along with the occasional shoplifting adventure.

If it is fitting, given all this troublemaking, that it would be a fight that would change his life, then it is also surprising how few of the details Darwin still remembers. His best recollection is that he was fourteen years old and talking on the phone when he got in a huge argument with Ed. Ed was upset about something. He was cooking and threw a pot at Darwin. Darwin stormed out and left the family home for good. He still doesn't recall what the fight was about.

But Ed doesn't corroborate the story and was shocked to hear it. "That's something I don't remember at all," he told me. "I was working. He left during the day sometime." Darwin's mother doesn't have a clear memory either—she's not sure if she was present or not—but she believes Ed threw him out.

Regardless, Darwin left. Most parents would be appalled at the thought of their young son leaving home to sleep on the street, but Darwin insists his family never tried to contact him.

He slept rough for a while, sometimes inside the lobbies of apartment buildings to stay warm. Soon he made the decision to leave Regina. He didn't have much of a plan other than heading for the BC coast, but that was part of the adventure. Try as he might, Darwin cannot now recall his first hitchhiking pickup out of Regina, but he remembers making it to Bassano. He found a campground outside town with a basic day-use shelter. It was pouring rain, and he slept on the wet ground in a wet sleeping bag and woke up in the morning feeling like a drowned rat.

Back on the highway he found a ride to Calgary, stopping at a Smitty's restaurant on the east side of town to fill his empty stomach. He left the next day, hitchhiking on 16th Avenue between 52nd Street and 36th Street Northeast. His first ride was from a guy who said he was going to Banff.

*Sure, hop in, I'll give you a ride.*

They talked as they drove. The man asked Darwin questions: where you from, where you going, how old are you? Standard enquiries.

*You got a girlfriend in Regina?* Darwin said that he did.

*Yeah, right!* said the man. *I bet you can't even get it up!*

*I can too!* protested Darwin.

*Oh yeah? Let's see!*

*What?*

*Let's see you get it up!*

*Naw, man.*

The man laughed. *Yeah, come on, I'll give you twenty bucks if you can get it up!*

*Naw.*

*Come on. I'll give you fifty if you just show it to me.*

*Naw.*

*What! Fifty bucks just to show it to me? Why not?*

*I dunno. I got too much pride.*

The man snorted at this. *Pride! Pride's got nothing to do with it! That's fifty bucks, takes you two seconds! And I'll give you a ride to Banff!*

*No way, man.*

The man pulled over near McMahon Stadium and told Darwin to get out. Shaken from the experience, he stuck his thumb out again in search of a ride. Another man soon picked him up, a big, burly, bearded fellow in a pickup truck. He was friendly, and they shared a bag of cherries as they drove west, spitting the pits out of the window. They chatted, and Darwin related the story of what had happened on his last ride. The man sympathized.

*Yeah, you get all kinds around here. But, I mean, hell, I'd suck you off.*

The burly man told Darwin about his first blow job, from a boy who lived down the street. For the second time in the span of a few hours, Darwin had to tell a man he wasn't interested in homosexual encounters. But the burly man was more cheerful than the previous fellow, and he gave Darwin a ride to the truck stop on Highway 22 just west of the city. The man wished him well before he drove away.

His next ride was from a very pleasant middle-aged lady in a VW Rabbit. His trip westward continued, but Darwin was simply relieved to be out of Calgary, which seemed to be full of grown men leering at him.

His path across British Columbia is something of a blur in his memory now. He recalls sleeping in a ditch near Cache Creek. He made it to Vancouver, but he can't remember how or where he stayed in the city. The real highlight of the trip was Victoria. Until he reached the provincial capital, Darwin had only spent a few hours or a night in any one place. Victoria, though, became the first city he'd ever explored at length on his own. It was a strange and exciting feeling of independence for a fourteen-year-old prairie kid.

While hanging around the Empress Hotel near the waterfront, Darwin met a middle-aged man who offered him a place to stay. Despite his two Calgary encounters with strange men, he accepted. The man took Darwin to his home and let him sleep on the floor. The next day the man was his tour guide, showing him the sights of the city. They got along quite well. That night they went to buy some weed. As they smoked together in the man's house, the man began acting strangely. Soon he was openly hitting on Darwin.

*I'm sorry, I can't stay*, said the flustered boy. The man didn't try to stop him as he gathered his things and left. Though he was still quite young and skinny and the man was full-grown, Darwin felt confident that he could win a fight against him if he had to.

He left and walked through Beacon Hill Park. Stoned and uncomfortable, he marched through the darkness. His eyes deceived him often: an empty area of the park would suddenly have figures standing in it; in the clear path ahead a glowing cherry from a cigarette would appear, startling him. Darwin's paranoia grew. He kept looking behind to see who was following him. He didn't want to sleep in this weird park, but he had nowhere else to go.

*All these gay guys. What I need is a nice girl to take me home. That's what I need.*

He looked back again. *Could have sworn there was someone following me.*

Darwin walked down to the beach and set up his sleeping bag. He laid down on his stomach clutching his hunting knife against his chest. His mind was wild with drugs and fear.

*Well, if they kill me, they kill me. And if they try and grab me I'll have a chance to defend myself.* The scared boy fell asleep with these thoughts pounding madly in his brain.

Darwin's pickup truck is parked outside the warehouse when I arrive at the yard around noon. Both moving trucks are here as well. No one is around. I notice the door to the warehouse is slightly ajar and I walk to it and push it open. Suddenly Darwin is standing a foot in front of me, looking like a zombie about to commit an unspeakable act.

"Jesus! You scared the shit out of me! What the hell are you doing?"

"Sleeping." He gestured behind him to a few folded moving pads laid out on the concrete floor. The deepness of slumber still hangs on his face as he stretches hugely and tells me about his late night at the casino. Darwin likes blackjack. Sometimes he does quite well. He did not do well last night.

I'm working with him today, just the two of us. This is a surprise, but a welcome one. Darwin and I have known each other a long time and our friendship is quite comfortable. Our personalities have much in common, particularly our calm, level-headed demeanours. Working with the boss also means that I'm relieved of my role as the Voice of Responsible Reason, which I serve as on most moves with Jesse or Keith. Today I can relax and just move furniture.

It's a day of small jobs: moving a garage into storage in Bowness; shifting some stuff around in our storage warehouse; internal moves in two houses, for a fridge and a safe. Work days like this are unusual but not unwelcome. The weather is nice, and we will spend a lot of time cruising around the city together. It will be a good day.

We take the blue truck and head out of Foothills industrial district for Bowness. We find the house, park in front and ring the doorbell. When no one answers Darwin tells me to wait there and walks around the side of the house. He returns shortly and says we need to take the truck around back. There, in the open garage on the alley, is our customer, an older lady whom Darwin has moved a few times before.

The blue truck has a side door and we line it up with the garage. We don't use the ramp. The truck is too close to the garage and there isn't all that much stuff.

The customer shows me what is going and what is staying. There's a wide variety of items: typical garage things like tools and paint cans, dusty old collectibles, wooden furniture, bicycles, bricks, and boxes. The garage has clearly been relegated to the role of catch-all storage for some time, but it will now be renovated and so must be cleaned out. We will take the keep-things to a rented storage unit. Much of the remainder will be junk-things eventually bound for the dump.

"I've known Darrell for years!" the customer tells me as I carry boxes to the truck. She expounds at length on how she knows Darwin, or Darrell, from his salad days in Regina.

Most of the boxes and furniture are of a weight and size that I can manage on my own. I bring them one by one, in no real hurry, to the side door where I set them inside. Standing on the ground, the floor of the truck is about elbow height and I expend very little energy bringing Darwin items to pack in the truck. It's a good system that flows well as long as I don't bring things faster than Darwin can pack them in, so I take my time.

The garage is cluttered and I have to interrupt our customer's effusive praise of the Saskatchewan Roughriders to ask for clarification on a few items. "This goes, this goes, and this—" she lays a hand on a vintage tall walnut chest of drawers "—is junk ..."

"This? But it's such a nice piece! Really beautiful." This is the fine game movers play: offering to take unwanted items without seeming to be shopping in their customers' homes. Sometimes we are offered pieces up front, but sometimes we make the offer ourselves. No room in the new place for that old armchair? I'll take it off your hands. Throwing out that old TV stand? I'll give it a good home. Half the time we sell these things ourselves for cash.

The woman seems as surprised in my interest as I am genuinely shocked at her junking a beautiful old piece of furniture. "Sure, take it."

She says the chest of drawers belonged to her husband's mother. A ninety-year-old unloved walnut beauty rescued from alley abandonment.

We continue loading, and Darwin climbs down to help me with the few things that are too large or heavy for one person to manage alone. Soon we are down to the last few items. I ask if we should take the large square reddish abstract expressionist painting on the wall. No, she says, that's junk. It is quickly mine, and she is grateful to have it gone rather than sitting in the alley. As I put it in the truck I notice the price tag on the back: $320.

The truck is loaded and secured. Darwin double-checks which storage facility she has rented, and he and I get in the truck and head up the hill toward Canada Olympic Park. He drives slowly and carefully and the customer is waiting at her locker when we arrive. The off-load goes quickly, about twenty minutes. The entire job has taken an hour and a half. Darwin settles up the bill, I thank the woman for her donations to my apartment and we're on our way once again.

\* \* \*

Darwin's hitchhiking story doesn't end with that frightful drugged-out night in Victoria, but his telling of it does. Though obviously a significant period in his life, the trip was over thirty years ago and the details strain Darwin's memory. He figures he stayed a day or two longer in Victoria, then headed back east. He doesn't recall any notable rides, or even how many there were. He estimates that the entire trip—from Regina to Victoria and back to his father's home in Westlock—took no more than eleven days.

When he told his father he'd left home and didn't intend to return, Darwin remembers being scolded. *You can't do this, you can't be on your own.*

*Well, I'm doing it.*

*What are you going to do for money?*

*I got a job at Dairy Queen in Regina. I'm going to find an apartment I can afford.*

Eventually his father gave up arguing. Darwin was determined.

His father's friends drove him to Edmonton and let him out on the highway. Darwin hitchhiked back to Regina and set about the business of establishing a life of his own.

He found a room for rent in a house behind the Hotel Saskatchewan. It was modest: though the $150 rent included meals, the lady of the house habitually went to the bakery to pick up free day-old bread.

He lived there until October when he moved to a house near Taylor Field. He'd started grade ten the previous month, working his job at Dairy Queen in the evenings to pay rent. But the new room didn't last long. His landlady had some rules and conditions if she was to rent to a fifteen-year-old troublemaker. Darwin broke a few of those rules when he snuck a girl in one night to drink beer with. The landlady confronted him the next day, and he started looking for a new place.

His next home didn't last long either. It was a room in a family home, and when the family went on holiday during Christmas they told Darwin he was too young to stay in the house by himself, a blow to his ego.

This life of young rebellious freedom was not going as smoothly as he'd hoped. Even for a headstrong fifteen-year-old, the world can be a difficult or even frightening place when you're on your own for the first time.

Darwin says his family didn't reach out to him or invite him to come home. When I asked Ed if he knew what Darwin had gotten up to after leaving home, he said "I just took for granted that he went back to Westlock" to live with his father. Upon hearing that the boy had not only been homeless for a while but hitchhiked alone to the West Coast, he replied "Holy Hannah!"

Ed also doesn't recall a time in October that year when Darwin says they ran into each other. It was a casual but amiable conversation.

*Where are you living? What are you doing? Are you still in school?* That last question, Darwin recalls, struck him as very odd at the time. *Of course I'm still in school. Why wouldn't I be? School's important.*

Around Christmas that year he ran into Ed's receptionist at the bank. She recognized Darwin and spoke to him.

*Oh, I hear your family's going to Fort McMurray for Christmas.*

Darwin shrugged. *Yeah, I dunno.*

*What do you mean? You're not going? What are you doing?*

Darwin explained the situation to her: how he was on his own, how he'd be working over the holidays to pay his rent, how he didn't talk to his family so he wouldn't know their Christmas plans. The woman was astounded. She left the conversation in tears.

It was in January that Darwin first met Ray. Ray was renting a room in his house and Darwin had found him in the *Leader-Post* classifieds. Darwin had plans to move in with an older friend and was only looking for something temporary. *Oh, well, if you're not staying long, don't even worry about the rent*, said Ray.

The house was in Hillsdale, a reasonable walk to Sheldon High School. Darwin rented the basement, and there were a couple more rented rooms upstairs.

One month went by and the place with his older friend never materialized. Darwin told Ray he'd be staying another month. *No problem, and don't worry about the rent.* Then another month. Finally Darwin told Ray it appeared he'd probably be living there for a while after all, and he felt obliged to pay rent. Ray started him at twenty-five dollars per month, which gradually became fifty dollars, then one hundred. This temporary arrangement would be Darwin's home for the next fifteen years.

Numerous other renters came and went during his time there, but Darwin was the only constant. Ray eventually built a bathroom in the basement so Darwin wouldn't have to keep coming upstairs to the shared toilet.

Fifteen-year-old Darwin didn't spend a great deal of time in the house. Each morning he'd wake up early and walk to school, then go work his evening shift at Dairy Queen. His troublemaking days were over, at least in terms of vandalism and break-and-enters. Never much for booze or drugs, Darwin's teenage transgressions were limited to bullying and fights. He was still a decade away from filling out his lanky frame with bulk and muscle, but that didn't stop him from picking on other students. One time he nearly got into a fistfight with a teacher, but backed down at the last minute.

Darwin graduated high school on time, aged seventeen. He wasn't an exceptional student, but the most valuable lessons of this time were not academic. He learned as a young man to take care of himself. The confidence and determination he'd gained would stay with him through life, as would an impatience with those less self-reliant.

His years after high school would also have lasting significance. Darwin hadn't much of a dream or even an idea of the path he wanted his life to take. In his younger years he'd wanted to be a dentist like Ed. But he came to the conclusion that he was more desirous of a well-paid lifestyle than any specific career.

He quit Dairy Queen and got a job laying ceramic tiles. After a six-week trip to Europe, Darwin found a job at a lumber yard.

These were idle employments, driven by a need for money and a desire for change rather than any true fondness for the work. But it was during this time that Ray planted a seed that would grow into something Darwin never anticipated.

When he was sixteen, Darwin had bought the Dairy Queen quarter-ton truck from the South Albert store. It was an old piece of junk for which he paid $150 out of a need for transportation. He did a couple garbage runs to the dump for people he knew, but it wasn't until Ray sold him his 1971 half-ton after high school that Darwin began moving in earnest, mostly junk runs for cash.

Young and shiftless, wondering about his direction, Darwin decided to try university. He had never been a standout in any school subject and he didn't feel much passion toward any career in particular. Opting for as broad a choice as possible, he enrolled in the business administration stream at the University of Regina. He didn't have the calculus skills, and he quit after a few semesters.

And why not quit? Nothing about school inspired him or gave him a sense of purpose. It was just something to do, something that might help him climb a few rungs on the ladder. Meanwhile, he'd been posting 'student with truck' ads and his part-time hauling business was doing well. Lacking a better direction, he decided to put his efforts into the thing that was putting money in his pocket at that moment.

He was mostly on his own in the business. There were no employees. Occasionally he'd get a friend to help him. He posted classified ads. Word of mouth helped, too.

Darwin was in his mid-twenties when he bought his first five-ton truck. Ray loaned him the money, about four thousand dollars. The truck was a 1978 GMC with a V8 propane engine that had been previously used to haul go-karts. This purchase represented both a progression and a commitment for Darwin: he'd never intended for the moving business to be a long-term path, but now he was investing serious money to make a go of it.

*  *  *

From the storage facility in Bowness, we take Crowchild to Glenmore and exit at Elbow Drive. It's early afternoon on a weekday, so traffic moves well on the freeways. Our next job is an internal move, meaning nothing will go on the truck. In fact, we're only moving one thing: a refrigerator from the house to the garage.

Darwin talks as he drives, telling stories. He hasn't looked at the address, but he suddenly turns right off Elbow and I assume he knows where he's going. But as he pulls into a cul-de-sac his anecdote devolves into muttering as he realizes it's the wrong one. He grudgingly interrupts his story to get out his book and check the address and we find the proper house not far away.

The home is large and well-appointed, smaller than an old-money estate home, nicer than a McMansion. Our customer answers the door and shows us the fridge, which is just inside the foyer. Darwin confirms that it's going to the garage and she says yes, and just then he gets a phone call. After looking at the number, he answers it "Darwin's Moving" rather than "Hello" and I understand that this is a business call that might take a while. I go back to the truck and get the supplies we may need: forearm straps, appliance dolly, ratchet strap, pad for the tile floor.

Darwin is finished the call when I return, tipping the fridge to test the weight. "It's not too bad," he says looking at the dolly. "We won't need that."

Forearm straps are strong woven nylon bands, usually bright orange, with three arm loops at either end. Nine feet long, three inches wide, simple, versatile, indispensable. Darwin and I stand on opposite sides of the fridge, each holding one end of the pair of straps. Together we tip the fridge backwards just enough to slide the straps beneath it, then set it back down gently. We have the straps stacked one on top of the other and we both slide the one on top toward the back of the fridge. Top to the back, always, for no reason other than consistency.

Darwin and I simultaneously pull our ends to the sides so we can compare how much slack each of us has and even them out. With the straps positioned to balance the weight evenly we crouch down and slide our arms into the loops. There are three on each end to compensate for height differential between users, or the length of the piece. We both select the top holes for the longest length and push the straps up to our elbows. All of this has happened wordlessly, the result of two men who have done this together many times before.

"Ready?"

"Ready."

Lift.

With palms pressed against the side facing me, my legs flex and extend to push me upright as the weight of the fridge rests solely on my forearms. On the other side, Darwin has done the same and the fridge hovers between us, hanging on the taut straps. We carefully manoeuvre out the front door and, as I walk backwards down the steps, I do my best to extend my arms and push the piece vertical to keep the bottom from hitting Darwin's feet and shins.

The fridge is modern but feels as heavy as an old model, probably around three hundred pounds. We round the corner into the garage and the customer shows us where she'd like it. We set it down gently and Darwin delivers the standard disclaimer: fridges and freezers should be left unplugged for a while after moving them to let the liquid refrigerant settle again. In this case, we didn't move it much, so an hour or two should be fine.

Darwin chats with the customer while I take our equipment back to the truck and sit in the cab. He takes a while to return and is speaking on the phone as he climbs into the cab. I wait for his call to end and ask him what's next. Back to the yard.

East on Glenmore all the way to Barlow. This is the third yard

Darwin has had for his trucks since I started working for him, and the first yard not in Inglewood. This one is my least favourite. The first was at 15th Street and 17th Avenue Southeast, a bit secluded from busy 9th Avenue but easy to reach by transit. The second was across from the Blackfoot Truck Stop, right on 9th Avenue. This was just as convenient for transit, but had the added luxury of truck stop amenities: washrooms, cigarettes, food and, most importantly, hot coffee in the morning. The current yard in Foothills includes a warehouse, which provides a warm place on cold winter mornings, but the remote location gives me ample cause to loathe it.

We arrive at the yard as Darwin's phone is ringing off the hook. He needs to take time to call people back, but we're on a schedule for our next job—another internal move, taking a large safe from a garage to a basement—so he asks me to get his pickup ready to go.

From blue truck to pickup truck: my new chest of drawers and artwork; forearm straps; appliance dolly; ratchet strap; wooden four-wheel dolly; two pads, plus the one I wrap my walnut beauty in. As I shuttle these things, Darwin and his phone calls move from the truck to the warehouse. I go inside to see what else he wants done.

A customer he has been storing furniture for wants to come pick up his belongings today. We have to dig out from the carefully stacked pile his two couches and two overstuffed armchairs. Darwin's storage operation is a huge Jenga puzzle in the centre of the narrow warehouse with tables, chairs, couches, desks, armoires, boxes, beds and more all stacked and intertwined in deliberate but chaotic fashion. There are no tags, no demarcations between customers evident in the mass of furniture. The only key to the puzzle lies inside Darwin's mind. He leads me to the rear of the stack and points somewhere into the centre: there. It takes us about twenty minutes to dig the items out and repack the ones we removed for their exit.

Darwin's friend, who owns the warehouse as well as the adjacent one, wanders over to chat and Darwin asks him if he'll be around for the next hour. He says he will, so we leave the furniture on the concrete pad in front of the door and head off to our next job.

* * *

Buying a five-ton truck meant Darwin was able to grow his business and do bigger jobs, especially furniture moving. He began advertising more. He printed flyers and hired the young nephew of a friend to deliver them on foot in the evening. As the nephew got older, he started helping Darwin in other ways, such as loading the truck. Slowly he would become a important part of the business.

But the most significant recruit of Darwin's Moving would be Barb.

When Darwin met Barbara Carefoot, she had only recently begun to get back on her feet after life had dealt her an unexpected series of cruel blows. At the age of twenty-six she was divorced with three young children, and charged with caring for her thirteen-year-old brother following the tragic deaths of her parents in separate incidents just a few years apart. Her family had been well off, but her financial stability was about the only thing in her life not causing her stress. Aside from single-handedly caring for four children, she also had to manage the affairs of her parents' two companies and personal estates.

To better accommodate her enlarged family, Barb sold her house and moved into her mother's house in the same neighbourhood. The new home was bigger, but also had quite a bit of excess furniture and junk. Barb needed someone to come take it away.

She found Darwin's card on the waiting room table at her friend's nail salon and called him to make an appointment. When he came to her house to do the job, Barb immediately noticed two related things about him: he was quite tall, and he was "extremely good-looking". Darwin did the job, and that was it, at least for the time being.

Not too long after, they ran into each other at a birthday party for a mutual friend. This time they had a chance to converse more, and Barb discovered Darwin was not your average Regina guy in his late twenties. "He was quiet," she recalls, "and he was very pleasant. He wasn't obnoxious. He didn't drink a lot. He was very decent."

Barb had more work to be done at her house, so she hired Darwin again. This time he left a broom behind (by accident or by design) and when he returned to pick it up, he found a note from Barb attached asking if he'd like to go for Japanese food—a new restaurant had opened but she hadn't found anyone willing to join her. Darwin seemed like the sort willing to try new things.

They began spending more time together, eventually beginning to date. Barb had three children and a young brother to care for, and she was impressed that Darwin didn't bat an eye. Most young men, in her experience, couldn't handle that situation.

She was studying psychology at the University of Regina, and Darwin's early taste of the moving business had finally given him a dream for his future: multiple trucks in multiple cities, crews working all the time, with him running the outfit and leaving the grunt work to his employees. It was a long way from his current position, with one beat-up truck and moving furniture himself with no real crew to speak of. But Barb thought his plans sounded more sensible than grandiose, and he seemed confident.

It may have been the first time Darwin had had real long-term life goals and a plan for his future career. After a while of drifting and dabbling without much passion, he'd decided to commit to the business that he'd started almost by accident without much ambition beyond making money until he thought of something better. The money was good, the work was there and he began seeing his business as something with potential to grow.

The timeline is a bit foggy, but after perhaps a couple years of dating, Barb lent Darwin twenty thousand dollars to buy a new truck. Although she had the money, the size of the loan speaks to the confidence she had in this man. The truck was a 1990 GMC. It wasn't particularly large by the standards of the industry, but it was certainly an upgrade. That was 1999. In February 2000, their son Axyl was born. A few months later, the family moved west to their new home just outside Calgary in the affluent acreage community of Bearspaw. Barb had too many difficult memories tied to Regina, and she was tired of living in her dead mother's house. She wanted a fresh start.

It was a time of change. Darwin bought another truck, a 1990 International painted with Atlas Van Lines livery. It was a solid machine, and big, twenty-eight feet long, a proper moving truck. He took it to Calgary and set about making his name in a new city. The GMC truck stayed with his friend's nephew—the one who'd helped him deliver flyers and later graduated to moving furniture—as he took charge of the Regina division of Darwin's Moving. Finally, Darwin had the business expansion he'd dreamed of.

\* \* \*

We snake through the city in Darwin's pickup to our next job in the northwest, Glenmore to Crowchild to Shaganappi. Darwin's map book is missing the needed page, so I navigate using his smartphone. Even then, the roads and streets are unclear, made worse by the horror of suburban naming conventions in Calgary: Edgemont Boulevard to Edgevalley Drive to Edgeview Drive (was that right or left?) and then you're on Edgevalley Circle, and it says Edgevalley Place is somewhere off of here ... but why does everything say Edgeview, shit, did we miss a turn?

It takes twenty minutes of Edgemont exploration and two

phone calls to the customer to find the street. When we arrive, she is standing in the open garage next to the safe we are to move to the basement. The safe is boxed in cardboard and bolted to a small wooden skid. We are taken downstairs to see where it will go. It's an uncomplicated job. The part that takes the longest is getting the safe unbolted from the skid with the customer's tools.

The safe is smooth on all sides and weighs close to three hundred pounds, so we decide to strap it to the two-wheel appliance dolly. Darwin grips the handles at the top of the stairs while I brace against the weight from below, and we gently drop step by step. The job is quickly done and I gather our equipment while Darwin makes another phone call.

When I get into the cab of the pickup I hear the end of the call. He's talking to one of his newer employees—let's call him Mark—who is giving him bad news. After Mark's job today with a mover we'll call Matt, the two of them were to return to the house of a lady they moved yesterday to try and fix a file cabinet she says they broke. Mark tells Darwin that they tried for an hour to find and solve the mechanical problem but failed. Darwin grouses at him for a bit before hanging up and calling the lady to cheerfully tell her that help is on the way.

"See, this is what happens," laughs Darwin, a sad laugh, a frustrated chuckle borne of displeasure I am well acquainted with. "I send these guys on a job, and they fucking break something." His voice is Darwin-angry, which is roughly equivalent to bewilderment for an ordinary person: Darwin doesn't get angry. "They break something and then they can't fix it, so I have to go and fix it. Every time things start going well and I think I'm making progress, stuff like this happens."

It's a well-worn speech, one of many variations I've heard over the years. Darwin often seems overwhelmed with disbelief that his business isn't blossoming as he had envisioned thirty years ago. In an industry where the core of your business is dependent on unreliable characters, you might as well be walking on quicksand.

We are already on the road heading to this unexpected job when Darwin realizes he's made an assumption.

"Oh, can you come help me with this now?"

"Sure."

He had told me we'd be done by this time today, but I have nothing to do and I'm grateful that he's driving me home with my new furniture afterwards.

The old lady lives in South Calgary, a rather central neigh-bourhood named long ago when it was on the outskirts of the city. Today, it's more commonly lumped together with Marda Loop. We find a parking spot on the street half a block away and knock on the lady's door. She answers—an older, tiny, sweet, kind woman—and shows us upstairs to the second bedroom where the miserable steel culprit sits in the closet.

Darwin tests the two drawers to verify the problem. The low, wide cabinet has a built-in mechanism to prevent both drawers be-ing open at the same time, as this would cause it to tip over when full. But something is preventing normal operation: sometimes one drawer jams, sometimes neither will open. We attempt to remove the drawers from the sliding rails, but they won't budge. We fiddle with it a while longer until, satisfied it won't be a quick fix, we carry the file cabinet from the closet onto a chest at the foot of the bed. Our customer leaves us to it.

For the next ninety minutes, Darwin and I attempt to diagnose and cure the patient. We use finesse. We use patience. We use force and aggression. We reverse engineer the mechanisms inside in the hopes of better understanding where the problem lies. Every eure-ka moment quickly fizzles. It is finicky work, small work. Darwin and I are among the most patient movers you could find, but our failure to progress is frustrating. I point out that the hours he will have to pay Mark, Matt and I is probably more than it would cost to buy a new cabinet.

Darwin doesn't want to give up. He doesn't want to let the cabinet beat us. He loses so many small battles in a week, accumulates so many setbacks that, in his mind, keep him from getting ahead, being free and clear, able to breathe and relax. These things add up and wear on him enough that he is repulsed at the idea of giving up a battle, however small, when his diligence should be enough to win.

But he knows I'm right, and we leave without solving the problem. The afternoon sun is warm as we make the short drive to Bankview where the boss helps me carry the chest of drawers into my apartment.

\* \* \*

The employee Darwin left in charge of his Regina operation—let's call him Peter—had everything he needed to run a successful business: equipment, contacts, an established brand and word of mouth. Had the Regina business remained as strong as when Darwin left it, his company would likely be quite different today. And, for a while, everything seemed to be going well. Peter took care of the work, managed employees and handled the books and paperwork.

But then, according to Darwin, problems began to arise—problems which strike me as typical of the industry. Peter began keeping the cash from cash jobs instead of adding it to the business revenue. He neglected to pay monthly parking fees for the truck, as well as the goods-and-services tax remittances to the government, two serious lapses that would later cost Darwin a fair amount of money to rectify. Just as he had begun to advance toward his goal, things began to crumble. The Regina leg of his business had become gangrenous; it was soon cut off. The old Regina truck with his name in purple lettering still sits in a farmer's field near the city, a GMC obelisk, a rusting monument to Darwin being screwed by his workers.

Before the Regina business folded, Darwin added another

truck to his fleet. Again Barb lent the money. Another International, smaller and newer than the old Atlas truck, with a plain white exterior. The previous owner was a man who was moving from the contiguous United States to Alaska. Once that job was completed, he had his son put it up for sale.

The plain white box was like a blank canvas for Darwin's imagination. He wanted a design on it, something better than the worn Atlas logo on the blue truck or the simple purple lettering on the Regina truck. He wanted something that was both his own and professional.

The image in his head was simple: a silver silhouette of a mountain range next to DARWIN'S MOVING in big silver letters. He wanted it to shimmer and be visible in the night—advice he'd received from a plumbing company who'd done the same with their trucks. But when Darwin went to have his design realized, he was told that none of the options quite matched what he was looking for. The decal company he chose only used stock options from a clip-art computer program rather than designing in-house. The closest they could come up with was a black-line drawing of a lake scene with evergreen trees and a cabin. Good enough, said Darwin.

And so the plain white truck became a billboard for the business: an unusual image married to an unusual name, professional and weird and memorable at the same time, not unlike the man himself.

# The Trucks

Anyone who spends a significant amount of time in a vehicle can appreciate the relationship that develops between machine and master. Wrench heads might know every part of their motorized baby intimately, but even the average car owner is familiar with the nuances within reach of the driver's seat. You know how to jiggle the key to start it, or perhaps you can work the radio without a glance.

A moving truck is different. It is transportation, workplace and break room all in one. There is so much more to a moving truck compared to an ordinary car, and we spend so much more time in them that the depth of connection between mover and vehicle is necessarily more pronounced.

The two trucks Darwin currently has are the only ones I've ever known. The larger one is a 1990 International we call Blue. The other is a 1994 International we call White. Though they are both of the same make and era, there is a world of difference between them, like two siblings close in age and appearance but with divergent personalities.

White has the lake scene on the sides and rear door and generally looks better than Blue, which was an Atlas Van Lines truck in a past life and still bears the large stylized blue A. She has had a hard life. Darwin bought Blue in Regina for around seventeen thousand dollars. The truck had been rolled near North Battleford, Saskatchewan, by an Atlas subcontractor who was using the engine idle as a cruise control when he hit black ice.

The cabs are well worn. White has two vinyl-covered padded seats with the five-speed gear shift protruding from the floor between them. The seats are equipped with hinges and springs for shock absorption, but the driver's seat is so loose that every bump sends you crashing into the ceiling. Driving White on Deerfoot's Calf Robe Bridge is the closest I will likely come to riding a kicking bull.

Blue has a single bench seat, which makes it easier to fit three men (a milk crate is used as an extra seat in White). The upholstered seat is covered with tough, hard-wearing fabric so stained and dirty its true colour is forever ambiguous. The stick shift has five positions, plus reverse, as well as a red switch that serves as the range-splitter selector to extend the gear options.

Both trucks had working radios when I started. I remember making cassette mixtapes to play while working with Ricky. The radios have long since stopped functioning and been ripped out. The horns, too, don't work, at least not as they once did. Both trucks have makeshift honk buttons installed near the ignition. I'm not sure what happened to White's horn, but Blue was the victim of Jesse's anger management issues. One day, stuck in traffic, Jesse took exception to the actions of another driver and began violently pounding the horn with his fists until it honked its last.

The truck cabs are filthy, the floors covered with spilled coffee and pop, the nooks and crannies and sub-seat areas littered with cigarette butts and roaches. Lighters are regularly tossed up on the dash against the windshield, and they often slip down behind the plastic, never to be seen again. Years of continual smoking are scorched into the plastic and fabric. There is no way for the cabs not to be filthy because there is no way to prevent movers from being slobs.

But the cabs are only for driving and taking breaks during cold winter months. The true heart of the truck is the box.

From the cab to the back, the trucks are very different. White's box is twenty-four feet long. Blue's is twenty-eight, plus a "kick", the part of the box that extends over the cab. White has a roll-up door. Blue has tall barn doors, plus one door roughly centred on each side. White has an attached steel ramp that slides into a gap under the truck. Blue has a detached ramp that leans unsecured on the back and rides on hooks on the side of the truck when not in use.

There are normally two piles of furniture pads on each truck. On White, they are at the back to one side, no taller than the row of logistics running along the walls about one metre off the floor. Across these we hang a heavy four-wheel dolly on a ratchet strap to keep the pads from falling over. Blue's pads are stacked on the wheel wells—fifteen-centimetre-high flat protrusions from the floor about a third of the way into the truck. Blue's pads are stacked high, six or seven feet tall, and strapped from the bottom of the pile to the top.

Standard equipment on each truck, regardless of the job: two-wheel appliance dolly; two-wheel box dolly; a few four-wheel dollies; ladder; straw broom; tools and cordless drill; rubber floor runners rolled up in a hockey bag; milk crate, also known as the strap bucket.

The straps we have are designed to hook into the metal anchor holes along the walls, known as logistics. White has only one row of logistics along each wall, which limits our ability to strap the load higher up. Blue has a range of logistic rows from top to bottom, but the metal has begun to separate from the wall in some spots. In general, Blue is in worse shape than White: more bent or broken things, more screws missing. White is recognizable and professional. Blue looks second-hand, beat-up, a bit the worse for wear, and the old Atlas logo is far larger than the Darwin's Moving text on the cab door.

But Blue has to be the favourite. It certainly is for Jesse and me, the two primary drivers and packers. Blue is better to drive and better to load, has a more solid ramp, has side doors to open in nice weather. Blue is bigger and can hold more, and the kick adds further capacity. Blue *feels* more like a serious moving truck. Ricky Roy used to call White 'Tonka' because it felt like driving a toy. Blue might not look as nice as White on the outside, but in the hands of professional movers, she's capable of anything.

# The Movers

After spending my first week on the job working with Darwin, I was introduced to Ricky Roy. Ricky and I worked together almost every single day that first summer. I think I had a total of six or seven days off in three months. When you work with people in close proximity and co-operation for eight to ten hours every day, you get to know them. If you get along, you become close.

I'd never known anyone like Ricky. He was a slick-talking dude, funny and amiable, difficult to dislike. But at the same time, there was a roughness to him that was plainly evident. He'd struggled with drugs and alcohol, and that struggle would continue for years to come. If I remember correctly, he'd recently returned from a stint in rehab in Montreal when we started working together.

Ricky was strong and tough. He'd worked for Darwin before but his struggles got in the way of being a reliable worker. This was another chance for him, and he was dead set on working for it. He'd wake up very early most days and lift weights *before* coming to move furniture all day. Ricky was a tough guy.

He was also a hell of a mover. It was Ricky more than Darwin who taught me the job: how to lift a dresser with drawers, how to high–low a couch around a corner, how to shrink-wrap a mattress and, perhaps above all else, how to make a beautiful pad pile. The moving blankets we use to wrap furniture are folded a specific way, not only for tidiness but for efficiency and consistency. Ricky took immense pride in carefully folding and stacking every pad, making sure the edges of the pile were perfectly straight. Darwin takes care to do this, too, but no one makes a pad pile like Ricky Roy.

It was also Ricky who gave me my first nickname. After a string of jobs with large pieces that barely fit, or that required me to squeeze between a piece and a wall, he named me Snuggles, as in snug fit. Don't ask me how his mind works. I think he just wanted to call me Snuggles in front of customers.

Oscar was also there that first summer. Oscar was a short, middle-aged Mexican man who spoke very little English. He was friendly and easygoing, a good worker but not a very skilled mover. When Oscar and I turned up at a job, our customers must have taken one look at us—a short lean man and a tall lanky student—and second-guessed their choice of moving company.

Jesse was another co-worker in my early days, perhaps the second summer I worked. Jesse and Bethany. I remember them as a pair, coming into my working life together, arriving each day for work in tandem. Bethany was a tough and strong mover, probably as strong as me or close to it. She seemed to feel a need to prove her ability and strength constantly as a rare woman in a heavily macho industry. She would carry lots of things at once and rush around, or go too fast when we carried a heavy piece. I didn't like moving with her when she did stuff like that. It seemed a stupid way to increase the risk of damage or injury.

But generally, personally, I liked Bethany and got along with her. Jesse took longer to win me over. He was a loudmouth tough guy. He grated on my nerves. He was strong, and a hard worker, I couldn't deny that. And it's not as though we disliked each other—actually, I think he liked me from the start. But I got tired of the macho posturing and ignorant comments laced with misogyny and homophobia he offered up. To me Jesse was just another guy who ran his mouth. My opinion of him would change years later, but we'll come to that in a bit.

The bits and pieces, the sporadic stints with Darwin over the years, the times I dropped in for a few weeks of work—these featured one-off co-workers, or recycled minor characters, or perhaps others I've entirely forgotten. It wasn't until the autumn of 2013 that I returned as a serious employee while writing *Rising*, my book about the disastrous flood that wreaked havoc on southern Alberta that year. Working three days a week, I was able to pay my bills and use the rest of the time to research, interview and write.

At that time, Darwin had a few regular guys, with Gavin at the top of the totem pole. Gavin was from a tiny southern Ontario town and had experience working for his dad's moving company. Gavin could pack a truck, and he could run a move quite well. He was also pure charisma. Tall and athletic with a deep voice and reasonably good looks, Gavin could and did charm every girl he came across, and presented as thoughtful, mature and professional to customers. I thought Gavin was nearly thirty, like me. He was actually in his early twenties, already divorced, with a burgeoning alcohol abuse problem. It was hard to dislike Gavin until you got to know him well enough for him to burn you. Once his drinking made him more of a liability than an asset, Darwin cut him loose—the only worker he has ever explicitly fired.

There was Gavin's childhood buddy Darren, who followed him west and worked for quite a while, a likeable hard worker eager to follow rather than lead. There was Geoffrey, the refined and gregarious middle-class Englishman in his sixties who constantly laughed and told cheesy jokes and was beloved by all, though he was not much of a mover. There was the other old guy, Jimmy, who was pretty regular for a while but then began turning up only spo-radically, usually for low-energy office moves where disassembly was needed. Nazi Bill, like Jimmy, had rotten brown teeth but was less refined in conversation. Lean and wiry, Bill lived in a camper on the back of his pickup and said so many horribly racist things out of earshot of customers—like "Gonna go to Africa and shoot me a whole bunch of nigger kids"—that I became numb to them. Dan was a short and perplexing middle-aged Franco-Ontarian who dragged his ass on jobs, insisted he knew the right way to do everything but spent most of his time disassembling beds and wrapping pictures, often frightfully slowly. Dan was pleasant to me and we got along, but he was often useless as a mover.

As these varied characters cycled through Darwin's Moving over the years, I began to recognize consistent traits among them. They didn't have much education, usually high school at best. Many had worked in other labour industries like construction. A few of them talked like they had other opportunities or better ca-reer prospects, but this generally seemed to be empty posturing. Most of them smoked cigarettes, and some of them smoked pot on jobs when they could get away with it, despite Darwin's strenuous opposition. (It's worth noting that only the worst movers saw their performance affected by weed. For guys like Jesse or Ricky, who are so experienced they can move furniture on autopilot, no ill ever came of a discreet doobie between load and unload, and I had no reason to believe any customer was ever the wiser.)

There were exceptions to this generalized image of a mover, but those guys never tended to be very good or stick around long enough to improve. Moving is the lowest rung of unskilled labour: physically taxing work for middle-of-the-road pay, around twenty to twenty-five dollars per hour. It is a hard job, but there are no real prerequisites or qualifications, no education or criminal record check needed. Just show up and do what you're told. It's easy to see how such an industry would attract men more interested in making some quick money than a long-term career. It's also easy to see how the high turnover and poor prospects for employees mean that Darwin usually has no choice but to take what he can get. It's hard to build a business when you're constantly training addicts to do a job you know they won't last in.

These are the people with whom I've moved lawyers, oilmen, engineers, professional athletes, media personalities, judges—the proverbial one per cent, served by the lowest tiers of the ninety-nine per cent. Despite the humble backgrounds or appalling histories of my co-workers, we have been in the homes of some of the wealthiest people in Calgary. We have handled their belongings, we have wrapped their beds in plastic, we have seen how and where they live. The dichotomy between this country's haves and have-nots is seldom made clearer than in the juxtapositions of the moving industry.

Eventually there was just Keith, Jesse and I. Keith has worked for Darwin on and off for a very long time. Now in his early fifties, he has a long history of crime and drug abuse, and though he is kind to his friends and usually a favourite of customers, he looks and sounds like someone you ought to be wary of. He can't legally drive and the only identification he has is an old Mustard Seed shelter card. But he is a strong and determined worker, and I like working with him.

Jesse has a relatively respectable appearance for a mover, not spit-polished but also not ragged and rough. He too has a criminal history, mostly between puberty and his early twenties. Jesse is a complex character. He has a lot of insecurities, some substance-abuse and behavioural issues, and these hold him back in life. But he is bright and friendly, bounding with an insane amount of energy and willingness to work, and is hands down one of the best professional furniture movers anywhere. He is caught in many of the same cycles that churn most of the movers I've known, but he has more upside and potential than any of them.

It's hard to say which is the real Jesse: the confident, capable, friendly man he can be and wants to be seen as, or the irresponsible ex-convict with a taste for cocaine and partying.

# Jesse

Jesse is that rare Calgarian who was born and raised in the city. His mother, aged twenty-one, married a man she'd known for three months, moved to Vancouver and immediately became pregnant with Jesse's older sister. A few months after she gave birth, her husband gave her a plane ticket to Calgary and told her to go visit her mother. While she was gone, he told everyone they had separated. Meanwhile, she discovered she was pregnant again. He told her it wasn't his problem and she should get an abortion. Young, single, with two kids and no career at hand, she was on her own. She took a job as a waitress to support her family.

From a young age Jesse saw himself as the man of the house, the protector of his mother and sister. His mom dated and briefly married again during his childhood, but Jesse still perceived himself as fulfilling the role in a way these men never could. He says his mother's second husband "treated my sister like gold and was an absolute prick to me"; his mother agrees with that description. The man was a disciplinarian and thought the boy needed the toughest, strictest environment possible. Jesse was, in the words of his mother, a "troubled" kid: constantly fighting, bullying, being kicked out of classes and schools. Perhaps his step-father's belief that a firm hand was needed is understandable even if it was misguided. When his mother divorced the man, Jesse was about twelve, an age that would draw a dividing line through his life.

The knife, according to Jesse, was a gift from his mother. She worked at a local store that sold Indigenous art, jewellery and trinkets. The knife—pocket-sized and decorated with stones—was a birthday present. His mother has no recollection of this and says she would never have considered giving her son a knife given his behavioural issues, which were already apparent.

In any case, Jesse had a knife.

One day at school, as Jesse tells it, he was walking with his girlfriend (an innocent relationship at that young age) across the snowy school field when another boy hit her in the face with an icy snowball. The sight of his girlfriend bloody and crying enraged Jesse. The culprit fled and Jesse gave chase. He caught the boy and threw him to the ground, demanding he apologize. Jesse says he was angry and upset, but also understood that the boy was just a kid screwing around. I interpret this as his plea that he was still thinking straight right up until the boy laughed in his face at the demand for an apology. That's when Jesse cut the boy on the neck and burned some of his hair with a lighter.

We like to imagine that our most important moments and crucial decisions happen in adulthood: perhaps our early twenties as we choose careers, or our thirties as we raise a family. But for Jesse, the moment he assaulted that boy would prove to be the moment his life changed forever.

He was kicked out of school and spent his time shovelling walks. One day Jesse came home from shovelling to find a cop standing in front of his house. Nothing would be the same again.

This is his telling of the tale, which I can't verify as his juvenile record is sealed. Interestingly, his mother has no recollection of the details of the incident that led to her son's first incarceration. To be fair, her memory is awash with years of endless and escalating bad behaviour from her son, who would go on to commit more serious offences. Yet it seems strange to me that a mother who seems so genuinely to care for her son should forget that very first of many occasions when her son was taken by the state, particularly at such a young age, and for assaulting another child no less.

In any case, as Jesse recalls it, his first stint in the Calgary Young Offenders Centre was in the neighbourhood of six to eight months. To anyone who might believe that our correctional system is designed to rehabilitate or scare straight, Jesse offers a different description: it was his "crime school". For a troubled young boy seeking a path in life without a father figure, being surrounded by older and more experienced criminals for an extended period of time is, to put it lightly, having the deck stacked against you.

Not long after he was released, Jesse began hanging out with a tougher crowd, older guys who sold drugs and stole cars. Aged thirteen, he watched with two friends as an older boy hotwired a car, which the younger spectators eagerly climbed into for a joy-ride. It ended with a police chase and several more months in kiddie prison for Jesse.

The pattern was set. Throughout his teenage years Jesse would have trouble staying out of trouble. Often his anger and bravado would lead him astray into violence. He got into fights. He pulled a knife during a schoolyard brawl. He spent enough time in the correctional facility to become accustomed to it before he was legally old enough to drink or vote.

Meanwhile the family had moved from Bankview to Altadore to Southwood, and finally to Erin Woods when Jesse was around fifteen. The two-decades-old suburban development was newer than Forest Lawn, which bordered it to the north, but it was not immune from the social issues and criminal elements its neighbouring district was and is notorious for. Jesse began hanging around a gang that called themselves the Crips, after the infamous Los Angeles gang. The most significant story from his time with the Crips is his break from them. It was a Halloween party, which he attended with his best friend, Chris.

> We were the youngest guys in their crew, lowest in the totem pole for sure. By the end of the night they were just looking for somebody to beat up. At the end of the night, [Chris] goes out the back door towards his place, I go out the front door towards my house. And, like, thirty of these guys follow me from the party. They're all guys that I rolled with, you know what I mean? They just wanted somebody to beat up.
>
> So thirty of them fucking followed me.
>
> All I remember was, I remember somebody was like, 'Hey!' and I turn around and I just remember this big boot, boom, right in my chest. I fell down on the ground, and I just remember fucking feet stomping me. And I was out.

After a hospital stay and extended convalescence, Jesse decided along with Chris to burn their blue bandanas, an act symbolic of their break with the Crips. As Jesse tells it, the two young men then formed their own gang, the East Side Mob, an organization that focused on battling with the Crips and selling drugs, and eventually garnered nearly one hundred members.

Whether this tale is mostly true or mostly fabricated or merely exaggerated is irrelevant. For what it's worth, I can believe Jesse's claim to have been associated with gangs and perhaps having started his own, the size, significance and level of criminality of which is up for debate. But even if he is exaggerating or outright lying, it would be worth noting the types of stories he chooses to concoct.

Being a gang leader is not a good way to avoid run-ins with the law. As his troubles continued and his eighteenth birthday approached, Jesse felt a desire to clean up his act. He'd amassed a lengthy juvenile criminal record and was eager to keep his adult sheet clean. Once he turned eighteen, he took a job at The Drink nightclub working as a busser. But some leaves are harder to turn over than others.

* * *

"This can't be right."

We're fifteen minutes early for the job. Jesse and I both arrived to the yard early, and he didn't need to stop for breakfast or smokes, so the morning feels oddly leisurely. But this can't be right—the address we have is for a tiny beat-up wooden house in Bridgeland.

The curtains are drawn, the lawn is unkempt and there's no answer at the door. Jesse walks around to the back of the house while I call our customer. I tell him the address we have and he corrects it: 12A Street, not 12th Street. We're one block off.

One block makes a difference. We swing our truck around to 12A Street and find a towering dwelling built into a bluff. A wide staircase of broken bricks and concrete leads up to the front door, nearly equal with the third storey of an ordinary house.

Before the job, Darwin had shown me the text messages from the customer describing what was involved. They were planning on leaving quite a bit of furniture behind in their old house, and the new house was only ten blocks down the street. Based on the limited information, Darwin guessed it might be a six-hour day, give or take.

Our customer gives us the tour. The house is quite big and there is a lot of stuff. They also want to swap the refrigerators, washers and dryers between the two houses, and swap a pair of couches with two at the wife's mother's house. There's also talk of a storage pod full of bins that they'd like us to unload. It's definitely not a six-hour day, but it's warm and sunny out, and Jesse and I are in good spirits. We're happy to have the work.

After a couple hours of loading, Jesse is still sprinting the twenty-six steps up to the front door and the sixteen more to the upper floor. I'm saving my knees, both of which suffer from chronic patellar tendinitis for which I wear medical support straps; they still feel good at this point, though I'm wary of their longevity.

I'm already starving. Looking at the mountain of stairs, it's no wonder. We are expending much more energy than on a normal move. My lunch is gone before eleven o'clock.

There are several dressers, beds, couches, desks and other large items, as well as endless pictures, paintings and other fragile pieces that need to be wrapped. Jesse and I debate the pros and cons of doing one or two trips. To me, it's a no-brainer: the destination is only ten blocks away, but we'll take much longer to load if we try to fit everything in, packing to maximize space. Jesse wants to get it all into one load. I don't know why, and it doesn't matter. He doesn't make a case for one load; he just mocks the idea of doing two trips.

It also doesn't matter because the more we pack, the more obvious it becomes that two loads is more sensible. If we tried really hard and spent a great deal of time packing the truck, we might—might—fit everything in, though certainly not the appliances.

We decide to get the big white couch on and then head over to unload. It's an unwieldy piece of furniture: heavy, long, curved, slippery leather and rounded front edges that make it difficult to grip. Slowly down the stairs, into the truck, a couple more small things and then our customer returns with subs for our lunch.

We scarf the food down like wolves and close up the truck. The warm sun has disappeared and the wind has pushed in clouds that look menacing. We drive down 1st Avenue through downtown

Bridgeland and find 6th Street. I pull the truck over in front of the address on our clipboard: a small, quaint, well-cared-for home a fraction of the size of the house we loaded up from. This can't be right.

A phone call to the customer explains that we again have the wrong address on our paperwork and are one block away. The new house, when we find it, is again tall with only fourteen steps to the front door. These steps, however, are not pleasantly wide but cut a narrow space between two concrete walls. This will be a challenge.

The storage pod is sitting in the driveway, but two boys of about twelve are already unloading it, carrying the heaviest bins together up the stairs. There are two hundred bins, and Jesse and I are pleased they are off our plate.

The unload begins with some of the smaller items we packed in at the end, picture frames and lamps and such. Soon it is time for the big curved white couch. Jesse drapes pads over the concrete walls of the stairway, lest we scrape the white leather. It's an awkward carry, terrible grip, and we have only an inch or so to spare on either side. Steady and slow, feeling its weight begin to slip from our fingers, carefully adjusting our grip as we move up the stairs together in practised unison, completely silent as we watch the walls.

At the top of the stairs there is an awkward zigzag: a ninety-degree left turn, then an immediate ninety-degree right turn to reach the front door. The length of the couch and the narrowness of the stairway means we can't make the turn with the couch horizontal. Jesse is closest to the door. "Going up," he calls, and I simultaneously drop my side down lower so the couch becomes diagonal. It's now even harder to keep a grip on, but I'm confident I can manage.

There is a man there, a contractor of some kind. He has been watching us, but now as we go high–low with the couch he springs into action, believing we're in trouble. "You got it?" he asks me as he steps forward.

"Yes, I'm fine," I say in a firm tone. But he steps forward again and does what I fear he would: he grabs one side of the piece and lifts the weight.

"Please don't help," I say with a touch of anger. "Let us do this."

"Yeah, he's fine!" yells Jesse from the other side of the white leather behemoth as he realizes what is happening.

The man releases the couch but stays very close, presumably in case I suddenly drop it. Because I'm skinny, people often assume I'm less strong than I actually am. But the last thing professionals want is amateurs trying to help do their job at a critical moment of concentration.

Back in control, Jesse and I navigate through the mercifully wide front door and set the couch down on its knees until felts can be put on the feet. We fist bump to congratulate ourselves on one of the more difficult carries of the day and run back down the stairs to the truck.

I feel the pain growing in my left knee. Going down stairs is always more painful than going up, and each descending step shoots hurt through my joint. The muscles and ligaments still obey my commands, but I stop and stretch a bit on the truck. I will have to be careful.

\* \* \*

Whether or not you believe Jesse's pledged sincerity of a clean start for his adult life will depend on your prejudices and skepticism. But the police are not the most hopeful of humans, and they were suspicious of a young man who had spent his entire post-pubescent life in and out of jail.

Jesse liked his new job bussing tables at The Drink. He liked the atmosphere, the energy, the pretty women all around him. He made friends with a man and woman who came in one night and struck up a conversation with him. They said they were from Edmonton. They were friendly. They bought him shots. He saw them again when they came in the following week, and they were friendly once again.

Once the casual friendship had been established well enough to allow for such a thing, the couple asked Jesse about buying cocaine. Jesse tells me he wasn't selling drugs at this time, but he knew people who did. In his mind, he was doing something harmless: giving this couple what they wanted, giving his drug-dealing friend some business. This continued over several weeks whenever he saw the couple at the club. Sometimes they wanted an eight-ball of coke, sometimes an ounce of weed. Jesse made it happen.

After a few of these transactions, Jesse started getting wary. He had no reason to distrust these people, but what if they were cops? He devised a test: the next time they asked him for cocaine, he gave them a bag of glutamine powder. If they called him immediately afterwards demanding an explanation, it would mean they'd tried it and it wasn't a setup. If they didn't realize they had a bag of fake cocaine, he'd be screwed.

They didn't call.

He was arrested soon after and charged with drug trafficking. He was released on bail and, while waiting for the drug charges to go to court, began selling drugs again to make some money.

Jesse tells me the following story. One day he was with a friend, selling drugs off his friend's phone. They took a break to go out of the city and shoot a .22 revolver that Jesse had purchased from a crack user for fifteen dollars. They spent some time shooting at cans and bottles before returning to the city and working the drug phone for a while. Then they went to karaoke night at a Boston Pizza in Calgary's deep south. Jesse left the gun in the trunk of the car with five live rounds and three spent shells in the cylinder.

It was night when they left the restaurant quite drunk and returned to the car. Driving down 162nd Avenue, Jesse and his friend noticed an extended Yukon with tinted windows beside them. Jesse was in the passenger seat and began exchanging dirty looks with the driver of the truck. This escalated to a mutual challenge to pull over and fight.

The avenue divides the suburban neighbourhoods of Shawnessy and Bridlewood. As Jesse tells the tale, the Yukon pulled into the parking of a convenience store on the Bridlewood side, and Jesse and his friend followed suit. Meanwhile, Jesse had flipped down the rear seats to retrieve the revolver from the trunk. He's not averse to fighting with his fists, but he stowed the gun between his seat and the door as an insurance policy—in case things got out of hand.

The men in the Yukon got out of their vehicle first. There were more of them behind the tinted windows than Jesse was expecting. They appeared to be Arab. Jesse's driver had his window rolled down and one of the men ran over and punched him hard in the face. At the same time, Jesse saw the driver of the Yukon come toward his vehicle with a sword or machete in his hand.

Instinctively Jesse reached for the gun. As the man charged at him Jesse raised the gun and covered his face. He pointed the revolver at the man and pulled the trigger. The hammer came down on one of the three spent shells, a 37.5 per cent probability that, had it not occurred, would have changed more than a few lives that night.

The man with the machete saw the gun and stopped short. He ran back to his vehicle shouting, "They've got a gun! They've got a gun!" The rest of the men climbed back into the Yukon. As they sped away Jesse got out of the car and fired his five remaining bullets into the windows of the truck.

He pushed his bloodied friend into the passenger's seat and got behind the wheel, racing off in the direction of the Yukon. As he drunkenly chased the truck through the quiet streets of Shawnessy, he struggled to reload the pistol, dropping the small .22 rounds all over the car.

The recklessness of what he was doing clicked in his mind at some point during the pursuit. His emotions cleared his drunken sky long enough for a moment of clarity. Not only was this incredibly stupid, but there was no way he wouldn't be caught. Jesse turned the car around and began driving in the opposite direction. Less than a minute later a police van drove past him, turned around and gave chase. Jesse stopped the car and police seemed to emerge rapidly from everywhere.

He didn't have a driver's licence. He gave the police a fake name, a weak strategy that crumbled when his bloodied passenger gave him up: no, that's not his name; yes, the gun is his; yes, he fired the gun; yes, the ounce of mushrooms in the trunk is his.

Now facing the prospect of serious prison time for narcotics trafficking and gun charges, Jesse did the only thing he could think of. He ran.

* * *

We've already named the day Stairmageddon. From the top floor of the first house to the top floor of the second house there are seventy-two stairs. Even if we conservatively estimate making that trip fifty times on the job, up and down each way, that's 7,200 stairs. By comparison, the CN Tower has the tallest metal staircase on earth with 2,579 steps, and nobody would be crazy enough to carry furniture while climbing it.

The unload progresses slowly, owing to the lengthy climb with each trip into the house and the sharing of the staircase with the boys unloading the pod. Jesse tells me stories as we work, the same stories he's told me a hundred times: how he tried to arm wrestle Hulk Hogan at Cowboys nightclub but was thrown out because

"Hogan's a pussy" (but also because Jesse was very drunk); the seven days it took to move Darwin's mom from one Winnipeg house to another; the time an elderly customer advised them to move a nine-foot couch too long for the elevator by prying open the doors and setting it on top of the elevator car (they declined). A Shaw technician arrives to set up our customers' cable.

"Do you know how much those guys make?" says Jesse as he shakes a pad out into the rising wind. "Like, a hundred grand."

"I know, you told me."

"Fucking crazy!"

As the move drags on, I begin doing the math in my head. We still have another load to get, plus the swapping of appliances between the two houses, plus the sofa swap at the mother's place. We're approaching suppertime already. I point this out to Jesse, and he feels the same: we'll work as long as they want us to, but we'll be here past midnight if they want it all done today.

Some visitors show up. Then some more. They bring wine and food, and some have kids in tow. As we carry things through the entryway and kitchen, we have to navigate oblivious friends chatting away, or hyperactive children who lack awareness, or—worst of all—the piles of shoes left directly in the middle of our path. What adult kicks off their shoes and leaves them in the middle of the floor in someone else's home? I don't mean in an untidy pile slightly off to the side. I mean *right in the middle* of the floor. One especially clueless lady left her shoes at the foot of the stairs.

People in our path we can see; small children and pets are trickier and unpredictable. Shoes and other floor-level obstacles are basically impossible to see when you're carrying boxes or walking backwards with one side of a dresser. Yes, we try to keep an eye on our footing. But throwing surprises at the people carrying your heavy and expensive belongings is not a wise idea.

Eventually the majority of friends leave and we push through the first load. The husband comes out to talk to us as dusk falls.

"It's getting late, guys. I think we'll leave the appliances and couch swapping for another time. Tonight, let's just grab the exercise equipment, master bed and a few other things."

In our loud, cheerful, tough-guy voices we tell him it's up to him but we'll work all night if we have to, whatever you want, we'll unload it and do it all again! He chuckles a bit and says no, it's getting too late, and secretly we're both glad he feels that way, too.

Jesse and I quickly get the last items unloaded and straighten up the truck only as much as needed to drive it back to the first house. As we're getting ready to leave, the husband comes back out and tells us we're going to leave the exercise equipment for today as well. Our job is getting shorter, and that's fine because it's already dark.

The customer climbs into his Harley-Davidson edition Ford pickup with his beer and his buddy and drives over to the old house with us. We park the truck while they go inside, and then we do a walk-through to see what stuff needs to get moved tonight and what can wait for later. For tonight: two big-screen televisions, a flimsy antique writing desk, king mattress, two red leather lounge chairs and about thirty picture frames plus assorted odds and ends.

The customer and his buddy leave Jesse and me to work. It takes us about two hours to get everything. The mattress is heavy, but the picture frames take the most time. We are so sick of those goddamn stairs. When we get back to the new house to unload, there are still a handful of friends sitting with our customers in the upstairs living room. The husband looks to have had a few. The wife is ill with the flu and looks tired, like she just wants this day to be over.

And then it is over. We collect our pads and floor runners and begin straightening up the truck. I go in to settle up with the customer, who has managed to talk a discounted rate out of Darwin. He gives Jesse and me each a beer while I calculate the math on my phone and give him the total: it's nearly two thousand dollars for a fourteen-hour day. He pulls out a thick wallet and counts out the cash, tipping us each forty dollars.

"Sorry for the lousy tip, it's all I have today. When you guys come back to finish the job, I'll make it up to you."

We drink our beers quickly as we chat with the husband, and then he gives us another for the road. We say thank you and retreat back to the truck.

"A forty-dollar tip, and he's apologizing. Fuck, that sounds good to me," I say.

"Oh, for sure it's going to be a killer tip next time."

(Indeed it was: we went back a few days later for another eleven hours to move four refrigerators, two washers and two dryers plus the couch swap and other items. The customers were extremely generous, putting food and drink in our bellies and more cash in our pockets. Jesse and I named that day The Great Fridge Shuffle of 2015.)

We finish folding pads and tidying, and then Jesse and I fist-bump and congratulate each other on the work of the day. He's walking downtown to take a train to a friend's house; I'm driving the truck back to the yard. It has to be me. Darwin asked me not to let Jesse take it because he doesn't trust him anymore not to take it home or leave it somewhere.

We confirm the start time for the office move downtown tomorrow, and he's gone. I get back to the yard around eleven o'clock. As I walk through the deserted industrial park to the bus stop, I sip my can of beer and feel the warm pain between my shoulder blades and a peaceful satisfaction that comes with doing a difficult job very well.

* * *

Tipping is, at least by technical definition, a bonus, something above and beyond the standard and expected recompense. In the food and service industry this has now become quite expected as a matter of course; not tipping at all is frowned upon as socially unacceptable. But in the moving business, tips are the exception and not the rule. For some people, tipping a mover who does a competent job is a given. I was never around on the many moving days of my childhood, but my parents tipped the men who loaded my belongings bound for Montreal, and I took that as a cue to tip the movers I hired after. Only when I started working as a mover did I discover the disparate opinions on the subject.

Some customers tip generously; others, not at all. Still others will offer us lunch or pop or occasionally beer, and consider that to be our gratuity. We once moved a Jesuit priest who gave each of his six movers two bottles of wine from his extensive collection. A few times I've sat down with a customer's family for a sumptuous home-cooked meal at the end of a job.

There are those who tip us handsomely for short and simple moves, and those who simply wish us well after an eleven-hour backbreaker. In speaking with many people on the subject (not my customers), I've discovered that quite a lot of people didn't even think to tip their mover. It had never occurred to them. To others, like my parents, one should always tip unless something goes terribly wrong or the movers are obviously lazy.

Some movers work for the tip, cultivating it from seed to fruit-bearing tree over the course of the day. Ricky Roy would declare to me en route to a job that he was going to get us a tip today. He would then be ludicrously personable and helpful, almost to the point of seeming annoying. Sometimes it would work, sometimes not.

Some movers think about the tip a lot. *Will we get one today? What do you think? She seems nice, seems like she likes us.* Personally, I never think about the tip. It quite honestly doesn't enter into my mind during the job, and if a fellow worker raises the question, I shut it down. You cannot foretell a tip. Hoping for it could disappoint you. Wondering about it distracts you from doing your job well, which is the best route to a gratuity, after all.

The biggest tip I've ever received is one hundred dollars, which I've gotten on several occasions. Once we did a multi-day move to a mansion on an acreage near Beiseker. The massive home was a realized retirement dream of an older couple Darwin had known for many years. The husband had made his millions in the energy industry, and his wife had a minor obsession with plastic plants. The job was many days long, but I worked only two. The first day, with only Darwin and me, there was no tip. The second day was the bulk of the move, six guys unloading a semi-trailer packed full of heavy and expensive furniture. The customers provided a hot lunch for all of us and their trades workers, and each mover got one hundred dollars extra for the day. The guys who returned on other days received additional tips each day.

The largest tip Darwin has ever received or seen given to his guys was one thousand dollars to split between himself and three workers. Per the customer's instructions, Darwin gave each employee two hundred dollars and kept the rest himself. I was working for Darwin at the time, but happened not to be on that job. My bad luck.

These are of course the exceptions in tipping. The most common tip is twenty dollars per mover, though I've also had customers round up their bill to an even number and tell us to split the extra $14.46. There certainly is no standard or norm, no customary fifteen per cent. There are no guidelines for tipping a mover, nor is moving always seen as a tip-worthy industry. The biggest tips usually come from more affluent people, but the wealthy tend to tip less often as a general rule. Friendly middle-class people who are appreciative of the work we do and care we take in doing it are the most likely to give us a little extra. I have no basis for this, but

I would speculate that those who have had horrible movers in the past might be all the more grateful and similarly generous.

Movers do not build your house but they are instrumental in helping to make a home. They take all your personal possessions, carry them to the truck, wrap them up safely, drive them across town and carry them into your new home. Many of these things are heavy or awkward or delicate, and many homes present challenges in their layout. Given the level of skill and labour required to do this job well, if your movers work through these obstacles with care and caution while being friendly, courteous and helpful over the course of a long, sweaty day, then to me a modest token of gratitude is a fine gesture.

When I worked full-time, a tip was extra pocket money, often spent on fast food, or at the bar on a rare day off. Now, as a part-time worker lacking financial stability, I squirrel away my tips with the rest of my pay. Those few extra bucks are needed and not to be squandered. But to guys like Jesse and Keith and many others, a tip is cash in their pocket. They can buy beer and liquor and cigarettes and drugs that night. Whether they spend it on vices or debts or food, cash represents financial security, however minor or fleeting. It's interest free and in their grasp. For the addicts it might mean the difference between showing up for work in the morning or not. But to anyone who lives more or less paycheque to paycheque, it is a tiny degree of freedom, and a teasing reminder of the happiness money can buy.

* * *

Jesse was facing three counts of trafficking a controlled substance, plus charges for possession of a dangerous weapon, uttering threats to cause death, and possession of a substance (those mushrooms in the trunk of the car). Despite the fact that the gun incident occurred while he was on bail, he seems to have gotten bail once again pending trial. After a breach of conditions charge two weeks later—he doesn't recall the details of that—the court was out of patience. On June 19, 2003, he was ordered to appear for a hearing to revoke his bail.

Jesse never went to court. He immediately went into hiding at his friend Chris's place in Altadore, above a little shop called Moon Grocery. Chris and Jesse were close friends. (Not quite five years later, Chris would be murdered and dismembered by another friend, and Jesse would be among those who had Chris's likeness tattooed on their arms in remembrance.)

Jesse's smirking mug shot was printed in the newspaper along with a wanted notice and brief description of the gun incident. His freedom lasted twenty days until he was recognized at Moon Grocery. The police were called and took him down while he was using the payphone outside.

That was early July 2003. From that day he was in custody until November, when he was sentenced to time served for the gun incident on the same day he began serving a five-month sentence for trafficking a controlled substance.

"What do you do when you're in prison?" I ask Jesse.

"Jerk off. That's it," he says. "Fuck, I read so many books. I bet I read over a hundred books. Worked out constantly. Smoked a fair amount of pot. Fought. Scrapped a lot."

His many brief stints in correctional facilities as a youth were only a prelude to a lengthy bit for serious adult charges. Being familiar with life on the inside helps only so much when you have to measure your incarceration not in months but years.

Those who believe Canadian prisons to be institutions of strict discipline and morality will be disappointed. Aside from the officially encouraged activities of exercise and reading, Jesse says the two most popular pastimes on the inside are drugs and violence.

We would have guys that would work out on road crews. We'd just have somebody fill up, like ... a milk carton, fill it full of dope and drive along the side of the highway and throw it out the window. Next day, one of the guys from the road crew would be out there doing his job, grab our dope and bring it back for us. That was one of the ways.

Another way, he says, was having his friend toss him packages of drugs over the wall of the Calgary Remand Centre in the middle of the night. He insists this happened twenty times, but I'm skeptical it could even happen once: how close could you get to the courtyard wall of a correctional facility before a guard or camera spotted you? Then again, stranger things have happened, and I can't completely dismiss the possibility of such an egregious breach of security.

One might wonder how drugs could possibly be consumed in a prison with watchful guards around every corner. Again, reality strikes down naïveté.

A lot of the guards would catch me smoking pot [...] in my cell. The toilets would have really good suction. So if you stuck your pillow over top of your toilet and you kind of pump your pillow, it would push the bit of water out so the toilet would be empty and it would just get, like, an airflow that would suck down, so you could just blow it into the toilet. Or else into the vent up top. [...] You could smoke cigarettes back then, too, so I'd just smoke a little tiny joint in my room and light a bunch of matches. I had a guard come into my room one time 'cause she could smell matches outside my door. I'd just finished smoking a joint. She came right in my room. She was looking around, smelling around. She said, "Stop burning matches!" or something. A lot of guards, like, you know are good.

I wouldn't even worry about them, I'd sit there and smoke weed in my cell and I'd know that they'll come by and see me and the worst they'll do is say, "Hey, fuck, be a little more discreet, man."

Then there was the time he made some homebrew while on the Serious Handling Unit (SHU) for getting in one too many fights. Fruit, bread, sugar, juice crystals—whatever he could get his hands on went into a plastic garbage bag with water for two weeks. Jesse spilled half of it on the floor of his cell while filtering it with a sock and paper cup, but there was enough to get him and his pals drunk for a night.

He did ecstasy; that was good. He tried methamphetamine; that was bad.

Some guy had brought in a whole whack-load of meth onto the unit. I only just tried it a tiny little bit that one time. Then I said, "Fuck, I'll never do this again." But that entire week I never ate so well. Because people were just giving me their food. Everybody was all messed up and they didn't want to eat. "Here, bro, have my plate!"

Violence was common, a natural result of locking up troubled young men together. Several times Jesse was sent to "the hole"—solitary confinement—as punishment for brawling with other inmates. But violence was not always the result of spontaneous clashes or settling of beefs: Jesse claims those prisoners with the most detestable convictions—rape, child molestation and the like—were pointed out by the guards, who would not only encourage him to "get that guy" but occasionally facilitate the beatings by opening for Jesse the airlock door of another prisoner's cell. I don't know whether there is any truth in this.

TAYLOR LAMBERT

One time Jesse's mother and sister came down to Lethbridge to visit him in prison. The night before they saw him, he called the hotel they were staying at. He told his sister he needed weed on the inside for social currency, and asked if she could bring him some. Jesse's mom recalls her laughing it off as an absurd suggestion: "Yeah, sure, I'll try my best."

The next day at the prison, they were led into a small room where they assumed they'd meet Jesse. Instead, drug-sniffing German shepherds were brought in and the women were strip searched. It was humiliating, and Jesse's mother was furious at her son for putting them in that situation, imploring him to recognize that his actions and life choices have consequences.

By the time Jesse got out, he was more determined than ever to stay away from crime. This time he held true, finding various jobs with demolition firms, moving companies and other manual labour work. As the years passed, Jesse never really found one particular career to dedicate himself to. He worked harder than anybody, but saved little and often had to scramble to pay rent. He liked to party and enjoyed being the generous benefactor of his group when he was flush—"king-for-a-day syndrome," his mother calls it.

And so Jesse's wheels spun during his twenties: Neither sliding back into crime nor advancing into productive society.

Jesse was working for another moving company that shared a truck yard with Darwin's Moving. Back then Ricky Roy was Darwin's main guy. Both Ricky and Jesse are strong, competitive braggarts, alpha males equally quick to laugh or to assert their dominance. One day a conversation between Darwin and the owner of the other company led to a friendly challenge: Which of their two tough guys was tougher? An arm-wrestling match would settle things.

They threw down some moving pads on the back of the truck and clasped hands. Jesse won, though Ricky was no slouch, and the two became good friends. But the more important relationship that developed from that encounter was between Jesse and Darwin.

# The Boss and His Boys

A psychoanalyst would have a field day studying the relationship between Darwin and Jesse. Fraught with tension and scarred with betrayal (on the part of Jesse) and mistrust (on the part of Darwin), the bond between them is nevertheless strong and genuine, sometimes as men, sometimes with a father–son dynamic.

Darwin describes Jesse as the best mover he's ever known. He is powerfully strong, ridiculously hard-working, experienced in the trade and friendly with the customers.

To Jesse, Darwin is a wonderful person, a true friend, a benefactor. He sings his praises to customers, or anyone who will listen, in the most glowing terms he knows. Never, not once, has his boss betrayed him.

But the inverse is not true. Jesse is a constant source of stress for Darwin. He is often late for work and sometimes doesn't show at all. He constantly borrows money on top of a long-standing four-figure debt he will never pay off. Despite Darwin's strong objections, he often smokes pot on the job, albeit never at a home, always in transit between load and unload. He rarely screws up on jobs, but the missteps outside of work make Darwin's number-one asset his number-one headache.

Several years ago, Darwin tried to groom Jesse as a Main Guy, a point man he could build the company around. He fit the mould perfectly: a total package of charm, strength, professionalism, ambition and experience. But temptations and irresponsibility always got the better of Jesse, and eventually Darwin ran out of second chances to give.

This is a typical Jesse cycle. He will come to work with a positive attitude and the best of intentions, declaring a new start and feeling great about life. He will power through moves, literally running back into the house to get the next piece. Each day at the yard, he will turn up grinning and early for work. His drinking and drug habits will be under a self-imposed check. This will continue for a few weeks until it all ends. Sometimes there is foreshadowing: a payday cheque, a cash job, a buddy's birthday party he's been looking forward to. Sometimes it comes out of the blue. We'll be at the yard getting ready, and the hour for departure will approach. Darwin will call him; no answer. He knows then that Jesse's not coming, but we'll wait anyway.

When Jesse doesn't show, Darwin has to work if he isn't planning to already. Darwin doesn't mind the work itself, but he's running a business and can't afford the time. He has supplies to pick up, job estimates to go to, emails to return, a million things that get put on hold to go move furniture. This is true when anyone fails to show. But it's worse when it's Jesse, because he could be the best. He could be the guy. He's supposed to be the guy.

The interesting thing about this is that Jesse denies it all. He's never late. *What are you talking about, I've never missed a day. Okay, maybe I've been a couple minutes late once or twice, but I've never missed a day.* He is adamant. His record may not be flawless, but it's perfectly goddamn fine, thank you.

On-the-job conversation with a co-worker is different from a sit-down interview with a journalist, though, and he shed some light on this when I pressed him.

> Few late days. I dunno, I blocked those out of my brain a long time ago. [He laughs, then pauses.] Serious, actually. ... I hate fucking up ... It hits me hard, and I fucking feel fucking horrible if I fuck up at something. Especially if other people are affected by it.

Is Jesse an alcoholic or addict? I don't think so. Does he struggle to avoid abusing his preferred vices? Perhaps. His mother, who is only peripherally aware of the goings-on in his life, believes he needs rehab to be free of the monkeys on his back.

She told me various stories from his life, examples of a behaviour pattern that undercuts his ingrained potential. But one tale stood out for me because it rang familiar bells. Though she'd struggled with poverty most of her adult life, Jesse's mom is now happily married and living in a comfortable suburban home generously purchased a few years ago by a brother-in-law who was flush after selling his energy company.

> And I'm pretty fricking grateful, let me tell you. So I thought to myself, Jesse's never had the opportunity to really better himself. He's stuck in that poverty thing, it's a mentality as well. You feel very bad about yourself. And I said, Hell yeah. It's his turn now. I am going to get that boy. I told him, you can live here. You can have the whole basement, you should see the basement, it's gorgeous, there's two bedrooms, everything anybody could need to live down there. You can live here for free. Don't pay me a penny. Don't pay for groceries, don't pay for utilities, don't pay for anything.

Just get your ass to school. Because somebody gave me that opportunity, my sister did. And I thrived because of it. The only thing I want you to do is you go to school and you study. You go to school and you study. Make it work. He got hired on with a stone masonry company [...] they seemed really quite serious in that they believed in Jesse to be very creative and they were going to pay for his schooling. What an opportunity.

He lived here, Taylor, for eight months. What did he do? Pardon my language: fuck all. He made a mess out of the basement, he had drugs down there, he had pornography down there, he ate me out of house and home. If I had alcohol here it was gone within a minute. He stole my car. Depleted it of gas. Nothing good. There was not one single solitary positive thing in it. I was patient for eight months. Tried to talk to him. He'd go, Oh, you're drunk. It just, I was hitting my head on a brick wall. I couldn't get through to him no matter what I said, no matter what I did. So I looked in the mirror one day and I said, OK [...] you're enabling him. [...] I got really angry with him one day, I lost it because I'd had eight months of this crap. I said, Get out. He wouldn't speak to me for a year.

In one sense, it's unfair and perhaps naïve to expect Jesse to possess the wherewithal to give up the bad habits and vices that hold him back. That said, it's yet another opportunity squandered, just like his chance at joining forces with Darwin.

Keith is a different story. He's known Darwin far longer than either Jesse or I have, working for him in large patches over the years. He and Darwin are friends, in the same way that the boss considers Jesse and me friends. When the yard was in Inglewood, it was a regular occurrence to have Darwin invite us to the Hose and

Hound for beers and wings after work, and he would pick up the tab more often than not.

For Keith, Darwin is more than a friend; he is a long-standing bright light in his life of darkness.

> I go to Darwin's, not always for work, sometimes just to hang around and talk. I give Darwin lots of free hours, man-hours. Just so I can be his friend and hang around and talk. And I'm not giving it to buy his friendship. I don't charge him because I want to be there. He's not asking me to come. I wanna be there. I wanna get away from people. I wanna go near that big goofy-looking guy who makes me laugh. He looks like a fucking hillbilly farmer, and he's such a giant, but he's so soft-hearted. He makes me comfortable. He makes me feel good. Even though he calls me names. But he always makes me feel good.

There have been plenty of times when Keith has burned Darwin by not showing up for work. But their relationship is more straightforward. Darwin likes him as a person, and he's a good mover and a hard worker, a favourite of customers. But Keith is not like Jesse, because Darwin can't envision building his company around him. They both have their own measures of unreliability and personal irresponsibility, but while a no-show Keith ruins Darwin's day, his expectations and hopes for Jesse always have farther to fall.

Of course, Darwin's aim is often drawn squarely on his own foot. Jesse and Keith and many other workers need money and favours constantly, nearly every day, even when they aren't working. Where's the incentive to make responsible choices when they can always count on free cash whenever they need it? Deep down Jesse believes, like many young men with inherent potential, that he will always land on his feet no matter what. Darwin's kindness and inability to say no only reinforce this delusion.

But the bottom line is simple: Darwin desperately needs skilled, professional, experienced movers, and Jesse is one of the best. He's so good that Darwin never really cuts him loose, even when he fucks up bad. Frustrated and angry, Darwin might not give him any work for a while. But come crunch time—too much work, not enough guys, high-end job with potential complications—he inevitably calls Jesse.

The story of a staff Christmas party several years ago illustrates their two distinct personality types and shortcomings. Barb and Darwin had a few employees and some friends over to their suburban home for a nice supper. It was meant to be a nice and generous gesture, a sort of thank-you for all the hard work over the year. They provided the food, drinks, and even arranged for everyone to have a ride home afterwards.

The dinner was fine and enjoyable. But the wine and booze flowed steadily and several guests, including Jesse, were soon drunk. After dinner, the group repaired to the living room where some good-natured jawing began. It wasn't long before they were moving the furniture to clear space for a wrestling match. Jesse and his old boss, who shared Darwin's yard, went at it as everyone watched. Barb was horrified, and furious that Darwin simply stood by without a word of protest. Darwin recalls:

> I was just thinking, This is what you guys do. You embarrassed yourself, you're not embarrassing me. This is what you guys do. I don't care that much. This is what you do for [fun], fucking go, I don't care. You put a hole in the wall, come back tomorrow and fix it. It's disrespectful, yeah, but I guess you just get used to it.

As the men began head-butting each other with a sickening sound, Barb went to her room, upset that the pleasant night they'd planned had devolved, dismayed that the industry elements she fears and hates the most—alcohol abuse and violence, which she often senses just below the surface—had found their way into her home. She'd long viewed guys like Jesse and Keith as dangerous, particularly around alcohol. She'd allowed them to come into her home and Jesse confirmed her prejudices.

Darwin's "I guess you just get used to it" reaction originates from a much deeper place than that moment at the party. It's bred of years of frustration with all of his employees, of seeing his grand plans for his business cut down time and again because of the realities of employing the types of men who are willing to do this job. Barb told me Darwin has a special talent for dealing with these guys, a sort of patience and good humour that many people lack. I agree.

But I have also seen plenty of giving up and defeatism. There's only so many times you can bash your head against a wall before you stop believing that the next time will be different. Maybe that crossed Darwin's mind as he watched the thick skulls collide in his living room.

I asked Jesse what he thinks about when we're working in the expensive and massive homes of the city's elite. Is he jealous? Do these things seem unattainable? No. He would like to have a home like that one day, and he fully believes it is within his grasp. He has a thousand ideas for making money, most of them get-rich-quick schemes or business plans with well-to-do relatives.

With luck, hard work and a personal reformation he might indeed have a shot at comfortable living and success. But he is his own worst enemy. Ultimately, his drinking and drug use are symptoms of a deeper condition: a deep-seated insecurity that prevents him from admitting his faults even to himself. A lack of self-awareness inhibits personal growth, and this is the key.

It's impossible to improve your life or make better choices when you've convinced yourself that you're doing just fine despite plenty of contrary evidence.

In my interview with Jesse's mother, she twice made comments about him dying young—"If he died tomorrow" sorts of things. I asked her about this.

> He's headed there. Okay, I'll tell you why I say these things. Because I've been to several of his friends' funerals. I've been to suicides, I've been to drug overdoses, I've been to a murder. These are all people his age and younger ... All preventable. All foreseeable. All of them ... It's only a matter of time. Unless he's one of the lucky ones that lives his life this way forever and dies of old age, because that can happen, too.

\* \* \*

We're to leave the yard at seven forty-five today, which means I had to leave my apartment at six. The No. 6 bus from Bankview to Centre Street Station downtown, then a southbound train to Chinook where I catch the No. 23.

Every Calgarian should ride the 23. The route runs between two LRT stations—Chinook in the south, Saddletowne in the northeast—and winds through East Calgary's lower- and middle-income working-class neighbourhoods. Housing is affordable here due to the proximity to industrial areas, and new Canadians from the Indian subcontinent, Southeast Asia, Africa and elsewhere often settle in this part of town when they arrive.

Coming from Chinook, the passengers are split evenly between whites and visible minorities. But if you board at Marlborough station in the northeast, there is hardly a white face to be seen. Regardless, the morning passengers are overwhelmingly male manual labourers, clad in dirty work boots and Carhartt jackets and bright-orange safety vests. The small handful of women headed for office parks are dressed in business casual and are generally black, Asian or Indigenous. This scene is no less representative of the new Calgary than ultramodern skyscrapers or the Peace Bridge or cycle tracks, though it's unlikely to be part of any promotional campaign.

At this early morning hour, no one speaks. There are no conversations between the broad-shouldered men jammed together in the seats. Some sleep. Many listen to earphones. It is late October and, like much of the year, Calgary is pitch dark at seven in the morning. We are tired and our muscles are stiff as the bus winds its way through Forest Lawn and Dover and Erin Woods into the Foothills industrial district where it slowly empties its human cargo. The women in dress pants exit near office parks and the men in work clothes shuffle toward industrial yards and warehouses and factories. My stop is midway down 76th Avenue, from where I walk south down sidewalkless 44th Street and run across Glenmore during a break in the freeway traffic. There, behind a two-storey office building, is the truck yard.

As I walk toward the warehouse I see the blue truck is already running. Jesse is at the wheel, but he is looking down and doesn't notice me. In the warehouse I find Darwin.

"Fucking Keith, man." He is upset. He pulls out his phone and shows me the text he received from Keith, saying he'd been up all night puking along with his young son and wouldn't be able to work today.

"Just another day, another day Keith doesn't show up," says Darwin with resigned frustration.

"Well, at least you know it's for a good reason this time."

Darwin looks at me with honest bewilderment. "I don't know that. For all I know he went home and got drunk like he always does." He goes off on a speech about the perils of the industry, how guys don't understand how the business works, how he had things to do today but now he has to go move. It's well-worn territory. I know it all by heart. I'm the guy who's never late, who never misses a day, so I'm the one Darwin complains to. He trusts me enough to let off steam in my presence at least a couple times a week.

But today it's bad. He's really angry. It's been a tough week and he had important things to deal with today, one of which was continuing the search for a new employee. This forms part of his rant, and he pulls up email responses to his Kijiji ad for a mover to make a point about the difficulty of finding reliable labourers. I look at the time; we should have left ten minutes ago, but I follow along with the boss as he takes me through the unfairness of his life. He does get screwed by his guys, but sometimes in these moments I push back and point out the ways in which he exacerbates his own troubles. Not today. Today I offer only sympathetic noises. I'm here solely to provide enough cover so his despairing seems more monologue than soliloquy.

My phone rings. It's Jesse, asking if I want anything from McDonald's. I didn't even know he'd left. I mention the time to Darwin and we finally leave the yard in his pickup.

We arrive at the house before Jesse and meet our customer. The house is a large duplex in Evanston, on the northern fringes of the city. Darwin and I do a walk-through; there is quite a bit of stuff and it will be a full day.

Jesse arrives and parks the truck. The morning air is cool and the day has a predicted high of sixteen degrees, perfect moving weather. Jesse and I are feeling good and we trade jokes and banter as we get to work.

He is packing the truck and I am working with Darwin to bring furniture out. Early on in the job, I begin to feel tired. My body feels heavy, my head is fuzzy, and climbing up the stairs becomes more and more difficult. I ignore it and push through the work. But something doesn't feel right.

TAYLOR LAMBERT

By lunchtime we are nearly loaded and the customer has ordered pizza for us. I am nauseated and light-headed as I grab some slices and sit on the ramp of the truck, but the food briefly helps steady me. We finish the load-up—which has packed the blue truck tight and spilled over into Darwin's pickup—and make the short drive over to the nearby development of Sage Hill.

En route we pass an old estate home, built at a time when it would have been a full day to journey on horseback from here to Calgary and back. Now it's a bizarre landmark among six-lane roads and strip malls.

The destination is a nice-looking but cheaply made home typical of new Calgary suburbs, a quick and dirty template copy of every fourth house on the street. As we begin the unload I am feeling quite ill. I keep working, but I can't hide it and I tell Jesse and Darwin that I'm struggling. Then, on a trip to the basement with some boxes, my body revolts. I make it to the bathroom just in time.

Darwin and Jesse take the heaviest pieces together and I run boxes for the rest of the day, dizzy and weary, pouring sweat and fading fast. It's a big job, and it is pitch black outside by the time we are finished. I fall against the wall of the truck and slump to the floor, completely drained of determination.

"Nice job today, bud," says Jesse. "Fucking tough guy over here." Darwin says nothing; it's not his way to offer praise. He's pleased the move went well and the customer is satisfied. I'm proud of pushing through the day and contributing close to a full day's work under the circumstances. I tell Darwin I won't be able to work tomorrow; it's the first time I've ever missed a scheduled day for him, though I'm giving far more notice than most of his workers.

Jesse drives the truck back to the yard and Darwin kindly drives me home, first stopping at the supermarket so I can buy all the food and supplies I'll need for what feels sure to be a powerful bout of flu. It will be a week before I work again, and two before I fully recover.

\* \* \*

What is the defining characteristic of Calgary? There are two ways to approach this question. We could frame it as seeking the aspect of the city that is most Calgarian. To answer this we might say a rambunctious spirit, or a capitalist's faith, or, god help us, perhaps the Stampede.

But the question could also be imagined as seeking a particular quality of the city that is ever-present. Put another way, what characteristic rises above the others to overpower them? There could be multiple answers to this interpretation, but I would make the case for what I feel is the truest if not most desirable answer: the suburbs.

Like any city, Calgary has a handful of neighbourhoods and districts with a developed character and true sense of community. Mission, the Beltline, Inglewood, Ramsay, Sunnyside and other such areas are found largely in historic, central parts of Calgary (Bowness and Montgomery would be two notable outliers). But for the vast majority of its history, Calgary has been an overwhelmingly suburban, car-oriented place in development, planning and culture.

Even those who spend decades or lifetimes living in Calgary never really get to know the city comprehensively. Most Calgarians would struggle to identify the quadrant many communities are found in, let alone try to label them on a blank map. Low density means that one million people take up a lot of space, and therefore have more district sub-delineations than other, higher-density burgs.

The size of the city is especially relevant to those who make a living in part by driving across it on a daily basis. Taxi drivers, emergency workers and a handful of other occupations are the only ones besides movers who travel far and wide across the city each day. Even having largely grown up here, I did not know the wider city nearly as well as I did after I began moving.

Calgary's communities beyond the historic core and a handful of annexations are all developer-planned suburban neighbourhoods with names that almost never have any direct historical connection to the area. They are monikers devised by industry marketers and sales people, designed solely to evoke a desired image or emotion in their target demographic. Thus we have neighbourhoods like Edgemont, Saddletowne, McKenzie Towne, Mahogany, Auburn Bay and perhaps the most egregious, Tuscany. Aside from the names of the communities themselves, Calgary has developed a peculiar street-naming system that might be quaint were it not so frustrating and absurd.

Within the community of Tuscany, you will find Tuscany Drive, Tuscany Way, Tuscany Boulevard, Tuscany Hills Park, Tuscany Hills Terrace, Tuscany Hills Close, Tuscany Hill Close, Tuscany Hills Road, Tuscany Hills Point, Tuscany Hills Way, Tuscany Ridge Park, Tuscany Ridge View, Tuscany Ridge Terrace and so on. The system is repeated for the sub-sub-divisions Tuscany Valley and Tuscany Springs and Tuscany Reserve. But at least the common identifier is a complete if arbitrary word. In Hawkwood, it is shortened to a mere prefix: Hawkdale, Hawkfield, Hawkside, Hawksbrow, Hawkview, Hawkstone, Hawkbury, Hawkville, all with their own internal assortment of Drives, Boulevards, Terraces, Greens, Points, Rises, Ways, Crescents, Circles, Places and Heights.

This linguistic monotony of a given neighbourhood's roadways is designed foremost as a sales brand. As a navigational system, it is remarkably useless and impractical, especially considering the method it replaced. Calgary's core and early suburbs are laid out on a numbered grid divided into quadrants. Not only is this the most effective layout for a walkable city, a grid makes it simple to understand instantly where a given address is located without ever having been there before. For example, 1234 8th Avenue SW is in the southwest quadrant on the 1200 block of 8th Avenue, that is, between 11th Street and 12th Street. Good luck finding 1234 Hawksbrow Circle with such mapless ease.

The suburbs of Calgary are something of a historical tour of the city's volatile growth and expansion during its boom eras. Different areas have different home designs, road plans, community layouts and models for commercial inclusion. Evolving consumer preferences, building materials and techniques, aesthetic tastes and approaches to urban design are all represented in a strange, uneven, outward-expanding visual timeline.

But most Calgarians don't explore the suburbs more than they are required to. The city has destination districts such as Kensington, Mission and Inglewood, which most locals visit at least once and often more. But what percentage of citizens have ventured through far-flung communities designed primarily to offer cheap homes, silence and security to their residents? When most people venture to other suburban areas of the city, it is generally to visit someone or to shop at a destination mall nearby. But this visiting can't compare to the familiarity of the districts and neighbourhoods of the city gained by seasoned movers, who normally visit two or more different areas each day.

Along with the fact that we are granted passage into private homes each time we visit a neighbourhood, movers have an unusually comprehensive knowledge of the sprawling city, from Forest Lawn to Mount Royal to Auburn Bay. Unlike the tradespeople and cable installers we sometimes encounter on jobs, we do not make comfortable money, we work in an unregulated industry and most of us are not presentable professionals. Movers, therefore, are arguably the section of the underclass with the widest access across their territory, even crossing lines of class and private property.

# Keith

Keith looks like a criminal. There is no nice way to say it. His face is worn and lined, normally accented with a stubble beard surrounding a thick moustache. His voice is as rough as his face, sometimes mildly so, other times descending to a deep, guttural growl and harsh rasp. He used to have long curly black hair, but for the past few years he has worn a short buzz cut to stymie any attempts to test his hair follicles for drugs. Wherever he goes in the city, he is regularly approached by those seeking street drugs, simply because he looks like the guy to ask.

Keith is short and lean, but he knows how to intimidate. He is well aware of his face and voice and knows how to use them to effect. When he wants to be, Keith can be goddamn menacing.

I like Keith. He doesn't scare me, in the same way that Jesse doesn't, because we're all friends. I can't imagine what I would have to do for them to want to harm me as they have harmed others. Most of the time they are both friendly, even a bit goofy, quite disarming. When Jesse wants to intimidate, he displays his aggression and evident physical strength. Keith isn't big at all, but he looks like he'd rob you, then cut you anyway, just for fun.

There are reasons for Keith's appearance, and reasons that it is rougher than Jesse's. Part of it is age. Part of it is that he has been to far darker places.

Keith was born in the early 1960s in Gooderham, Ontario, a two-and-a-half-hour drive northeast of Toronto in Haliburton County. His father was a truck driver who left the family before Keith knew him. His mother was the head of housekeeping at a resort camp. Both of his parents came from white supremacist families, and Keith was raised believing he was at the top of a racial hierarchy.

When Keith was still young, his mother remarried and they moved to the outskirts of Toronto. Her new husband was a friendly, hard-working, well-liked man who was a good provider for the family. One night Keith awoke to find his step-father raping him. He was seven years old.

The abuse continued for years, and Keith's two older sisters were victims as well. The siblings discussed the horrors with each other but no one else, for fear their abuser would make good on his threat to hurt their mother if they spoke up. The cruelty was not only sexual. The step-father was often violent toward the children, with regular beatings as punishment for any perceived faults. As Keith recalls, his mother did nothing to stop the violence or psychological abuse her husband openly perpetrated on her children. He never asked her before she died, but he figures she was scared of losing her provider.

After three years of regular abuse, the kids told their mom they were being raped. She didn't believe them and accused them of lying. Around this time, Keith and his sisters began smoking marijuana, which they initially stole from their uncle's stash. Keith was desperate for something to take him away, something to help him escape his horrible thoughts. Nightmares envenomed his sleep.

A child's imagination is both magical and foundational in human development, but it can also be poisoned. Keith and his sisters hated their tormentor so much that they began thinking of ways to kill him. One day they came home and saw his jacket hanging with the others in the stairwell. They knew he was asleep because he worked nights. The kids set fire to the jackets and went outside to sit and watch. They hoped if the blaze started in the stairwell, their step-father's exit would be blocked. Much of the house was destroyed, and they were never caught, but their abuser survived. At ten years old, Keith was an attempted murderer.

The pot was a minor help, but there was also booze. The step-father would often give the kids beers as a prelude to abuse. For nine- and ten-year-olds, this was pretty cool rule-breaking, even though they knew what inevitably came after.

Eventually, their mom believed their story and left the step-father. As far as Keith can recall, the man was convicted and served time, but he's not sure. It didn't matter. The abuse had stopped, but the damage was done and the horrors lived inside them now, in their thoughts and nightmares. Every moment of every day, Keith would be haunted by the memories of what had been done to him. Hurt and confusion evolved into anger and began festering inside him. He began seeking anything that would subdue his internal demons.

By his mid-teens, the family was back in Haliburton County and Keith was using cocaine, mushrooms and LSD. He was getting into trouble, though in small-town Ontario there was nothing too serious to get into: aside from drugs and petty crime, boosting cars to drive to bush parties was as bad as it got.

The psychological damage inflicted by the abuse had carved him into a jaded young man angry at the world who had long since stopped caring about anything and anyone. He believed no one cared about him. Physical violence from his mother and her new boyfriends continued. School meant nothing to him and his performance reflected that. In grade nine, Keith dropped out, left home and went to Toronto.

He found a job sorting automotive parts for $4.35 an hour. He loved the freedom, the ability to go anywhere and do anything he pleased. Without a place of his own, he lived on the streets, occasionally staying with his grandmother or friends. Drugs and poverty and petty crime were his life, and he dove head first into a dark world he would remain in for more than two years. It was during this period that he began using heroin, which took his pain and terrible thoughts away like nothing before. It was the perfect drug, and he used it every day.

Keith moved back home after his mother married her third husband, but he stayed only a few months before he moved back to Toronto to be with Judy.

Judy was a friend from his school days. With both Keith's mother and step-father gone to work early in the morning, Keith often slept in or skipped school. His mother hired Judy as something of a minder for him. She would come over and make sure he was up and they would walk to school together. She became his first girlfriend, and Keith's family was sure that the level-headed girl was just the influence he needed. They spent much of their free time together. He introduced her to marijuana.

Years later, when Keith followed Judy back to Toronto, he moved in with her family. Judy became pregnant and the couple had to find their own place. Soon enough, they were engaged.

On the day of his wedding, Keith woke up with a hangover from a night of drinking and went to work at his landscaping job. He had forgotten what day it was. With everyone gathered at Judy's parents' house, Keith got a frantic phone call from his mother. He left work and raced over.

I showed up, I was in construction boots, pair of cut-off jeans and a t-shirt ... And the worst part was, I

dropped a tab of acid that morning. So I was just fucking zooed. [Laugh]

Judy was not impressed. But if that was the worst story of their
relationship, they might have been able to laugh about it in time.
Instead, their marriage fell further into darkness.

At first Judy didn't know that Keith was using heroin. He was
shooting up every day, beginning first thing in the morning when
he went to the bathroom. According to Keith, he was high so often that people became suspicious of his appearance and behaviour
only when he was sober.

It was money, or rather the mysterious lack of it, that became
the loose thread that unravelled everything. They were both working—Keith as a landscaper, Judy as a part-time server at the University of Toronto's German Club—but finding money for rent or
food always seemed to be a struggle. It was like swimming against
a current in a still pool. It didn't make sense.

As [with] all addicts, drugs are a priority in your life.
And then when it comes down to the crunch time, "Oh
yeah, I gotta pay rent this month." You start remembering things you actually should have been banking for.

They fought about money often. Judy demanded to know
where it all went. Keith's answers were vague and non-specific and
didn't satisfy her. His pot habit was no secret, but she'd ask how he
spent five hundred dollars if the ounce cost only fifty dollars. If she
bought something, he'd sell it for cash. If she had cash, he'd steal it.

One morning a typical argument from the previous night heat-
ed up again.

I just said, "You know what? I'll be fucking back in
a minute."

Twenty minutes later I come home, and I drop just over nine thousand dollars on the table. "There you go, baby. Can I have a little bit?" She gave me a couple hundred dollars. Of course, I'd steal it from her when I needed the money. But she was happy. She kept bugging me, "Where'd it come from, where'd you get it?"

Where he'd gotten it was the Bank of Nova Scotia around the corner. Keith says the decision to go rob it that day was spur of the moment, but he'd had the plan in the works for a while. Someone had told him that Bank of Nova Scotia branches had fake security cameras—remember, this was the early 1980s. It had taken a day or so to get a gun, which Keith kept hidden as he walked into the bank unmasked. He approached a teller and discreetly revealed the gun.

I just said, "Gimme the cash or I'm gonna fucking shoot you, bitch." I said those exact words. And she gave me some cash. Turned out it was almost ten grand in cash she gave me. And just that alone, the amount of money I got and knowing that I had that power and could actually scare somebody that much and make them do what I wanted them to, I felt like a god for a minute.

Judy pressed Keith on where the money came from, but he brushed her aside. It was only later that night when he was drunk that he said what he'd done. He thought she seemed impressed by his fearlessness. Later he learned how scared she was living with a man—her husband, the father of her children—who had no qualms about using the threat of violence to get what he wanted.

The money gave them breathing room, but Keith's surreptitious drug habit was the hole in the bucket that leaked it away. A few months later he robbed a different branch of the same bank in the same way for four thousand dollars. Both times he got away with it, in the sense that the police wouldn't have caught him on their own. They were flush again, but the bucket continued to leak and the money was quickly gone. Keith started selling drugs. The junkie in him needed to find the quickest, easiest path to resources to buy more dope.

Lesser crimes, relative to armed robberies, are scattered throughout this period of his life. Keith says he and the guys he ran with would regularly boost cars from dealerships due to their poor security measures and lack of camera surveillance. When they finished with the vehicles, they'd simply dump them in the Humber River for a forensic evidence rinse.

> Just off of Scarlet Road and Dundas [...] the Humber River runs below that, but it's fairly deep. And you can drive a car in. Yeah, you're going to get a little wet yourself, whatever, doesn't matter ... Just dump the fucking car, walk away. Sorry about their luck. They're insured. I bet you I've done that fifteen, twenty times, throwing cars in the river. The worst part about doing that was, they've got, it was called a lamprey fish, like a snake fish. It's full of teeth. What they do is when they got you, they just bore a hole right through your body, they don't come off easy ... Fucking hated going in that river then.

All the while tension and distrust were fraying Keith's relationship with Judy. (He sees this now, with the benefit of hindsight made clear by years of therapy and counselling. At the time, the fog of addiction obscured the bright lights of his wife and children.) Money was tight, and Judy had figured out Keith's heroin habit.

She would beg Keith to go clean, to give up both drugs and crime, but any effort he made withered after a day or two. Finally she made a stand.

During an argument, Judy said she was taking the children and leaving. Keith didn't like that. He tried to reason with her, to make her understand. She was adamant. He didn't like that either.

> A little pain makes people understand stuff. So I grabbed her right ear, and I almost ripped it off her fucking head. I started just twisting it, and she's still telling me how she's leaving, and I just kept more and more and more. Until finally it did crack, like, I broke the skin from actually just in my hand turning her fucking ear. I was just trying to let her understand: I will fucking hurt you if you take my kids.

As Keith recalls, "things calmed down" after that—meaning Judy kept her mouth shut and stayed put, probably terrified. But not long after she again screwed up the courage to say she was leaving. This time, her husband reminded her that he had a gun. He told her he'd kill her if she left: "'If you take me to court, make sure they bring you body protection. Because I'm going to walk in that courtroom and I'll put a bullet right in your fucking head before I say a word.'"

Judy went to the police. She told them about the robberies. Keith had told her enough of the details that her story was credible. One afternoon, Keith pulled into the driveway. The moment he switched the car off, they swarmed him and dragged him out. He remembers his children standing on the front porch with Judy. She was yelling: I love you, I am so sorry, but this is what you need.

> I spent the first fucking year and a half planning in my head how to get rid of her body. And then after that,

I wasn't so far into the drugs, my brain was starting to actually function again. I realized what I'd done to myself, nobody did it to me ... I actually started falling more in love with her. And I know this might sound stupid, but it's thirty years later and I love her more today than the day I married her.

* * *

Keith and I are on our second job of the day: picking up a large tabletop and taking it to a shop for repairs. Our customer is a very wealthy one Keith has moved before. The house is beautiful, ostentatious in its size, deliberate in its grandeur of scale, a huge throbbing erection of a dwelling. The low hitch of our truck won't let us back into the driveway so I park on the street and we walk to the door. The driveway seems large enough to host an NBA game.

We ring the bell. The double doors before us are close to three metres tall. One door opens and the lady of the house appears. She says hello and I stick out my hand and begin to introduce myself. But she cuts me off as she looks past me. "That truck is too big!" she gasps. "You aren't charging me extra for that big truck, are you?" For a moment I imagine that she must be joking, but her tone of voice and demeanour are serious, even concerned.

I lower my awkwardly outstretched hand that she has ignored. "No, no," I say with a laugh, "of course not." Reassured, she then turns and walks inside, and we follow. The table—which is longer than some rooms in my apartment—is just off the foyer in the dining room. We examine it, and she tells us that only the tabletop is going. I go out to get pads, tools and runners while Keith chats with the customer, who remembers him from their previous move.

I return and lay a pad down near the table. Keith calls from the kitchen using the nickname given to me by my Polish girl-friend, which is easier for him to remember than my actual name because of my moustache.

"Hey Staś! Come here, you gotta see this house." I walk around the corner and find myself in the enormous main living area of the house, one massive open area comprising kitchen, living room and eating area. The span across this room is close to twenty metres. The kitchen has two islands with marble tops. Keith lavishes gruff praise upon the home, and our customer remarks about the never-ending chore of interior decorating. "My favourite part," says Keith, "is the golf simulator downstairs."

The customer laughs and Keith tells me how huge and amazing it is as I lead him back to the job: the dining room table. He crawls under it and removes the sixteen screws holding the tabletop to the lower frame. I spread two pads beside the table so we can set it on edge, and floor runners leading to the door so we can walk through the house with our shoes on. As we work, the customer watches us closely.

"You guys aren't going to go for lunch and bill me for it, are you?"

I smile and cheerfully assure her that we'll be going straight to our destination. Her question is insulting—and baffling, since she's hired Darwin several times, a sign of trust—but I have to remain professional.

Keith and I tip the detached tabletop onto the pad on the ground. We manage to heave it up into our hands, carrying it on its long edge. It is quite heavy, probably close to four hundred fifty pounds, as well as unwieldy in length and height. We carefully manoeuvre it out of the house and make the long trek across the driveway to the truck, where we set it on pads and strap it to the wall.

Before we leave, the customer gives us two hundred dollars in cash and a handwritten receipt for the repairman to sign, acknowledging that he has received both the table and this deposit for his work. Once he signs it, we are to keep the document until we pick up the table next week.

TAYLOR LAMBERT

"I found this guy on Kijiji," she explains, "so I can't really trust him."

As we drive away Keith tells me that she made her fortune by founding a chain of payday-loan stores. This does not endear her to me further.

I convey my negative thoughts on our customer—this obscenely wealthy woman who is so concerned with every penny of her fortune that she thinks little of insulting Keith and me—to both Darwin and Keith. They both stick up for her.

"Maybe she was just having a bad day or something," says Darwin.

\* \* \*

Since this book is in part an exploration of class, it's important for the reader to know who is leading the exploration, even at this late juncture. Let me introduce myself more fully. I am a thirty-year-old white middle-class Canadian male. I was born in Regina and grew up there and in Calgary, moving back and forth several times before I started grade seven in Calgary, where I would remain until finishing high school.

My father comes from rural Polish–Canadian stock. He grew up on the isolated family farm in Saskatchewan, where they did not have electricity until he was old enough to shoot a rifle. As a young man he attended technical college and eventually went on to a long career in information-technology sales.

My mother is the first-born child of German post-war immigrants who met and married in Saskatchewan. Her father ran a successful auto body shop in Regina with his brother, and the family was comfortable: two cars, a bungalow in the suburbs and a lakefront cottage for the weekends.

When my parents first married, money was tight and they lived in an apartment, slowly but steadily climbing the ladder of financial security and comfort. My mom put her dreams of a career in medicine on hold for many years to take care of me and my younger sister. But my dad's job more than provided for our family, and I would describe my youth as comfortable suburban middle class, though our branch of the family tree was not far removed from our ancestral struggles of war and life on the land. That my sister and I were fairly free of want was not only due to our parents but also because our grandparents had endeavoured to give their descendants more opportunity than they had known, and we were always aware of how much harder than ours their lives had been.

At some point around the completion of my high school years, I began feeling differently about things like wealth and comfort. Perhaps it was the prospect of pursuing a career I cared little about solely to earn money and maintain a lifestyle. Perhaps it was something else. I began rejecting my middle-class roots in favour of ... well, I wasn't sure. But I did know that making lots of money and having cool stuff genuinely weren't important to me. I was a bright kid with good marks and I probably could have gone into almost any field I desired. In choosing journalism as a career I was knowingly forgoing job security and a lucrative salary in favour of idealism, intellectual endeavours and a vague notion of service.

Aside from my years living as a typical poor independent student and travelling the world on a shoestring, I had decent-paying salaried positions with several newspapers before deciding to freelance full-time in 2012. As unprofitable as this decision was, I only worsened my financial position by choosing to write books, which have a terribly poor return for such an enormous time commitment. And so I became, to the best of my knowledge, Calgary's only journalist/author/mover.

I live below the poverty line. I get my taxes back and qualify for subsidized services such as a cheap transit pass. I wasn't born in this income bracket, nor did I end up here through error. It was a sacrifice I was willing to make to follow the career path I believed in.

I make less money than Keith or Jesse—who both work full-time—and yet I live reasonably well and even manage to slowly grow my savings. My diet is largely vegetarian due to affordability, but I learned to cook a wide variety of Indian food during my time in that country, and so it is hardly a burden. I drink, but in moderation, rarely at bars and not every night. Cigarettes, that great tax on the poor, are no longer a drain on my finances; I can't imagine shelling out hundreds of dollars each month and still keeping my head above water.

Do not mistake my intention here: I generally stand as a bleeding-heart lefty on social issues, and I am loath to blame poor people for being poor. My point is that the money that Keith and Jesse earn from moving is more than enough to comfortably get by and perhaps even advance in life. It is not necessarily lack of income that holds them back. They are not lazy men; they work hard labour nearly every day of their lives, and Jesse in particular seems to have bottomless stores of energy. So why do they struggle while I gain ground? Is it the choices I make? Or the fact that I'm able to make them?

\* \* \*

The case against Keith was so overwhelming that his lawyer advised him to confess to the robberies in hope of leniency. He was sentenced to seven years in prison, to be served at Millhaven Institute. Fortunately, his brother was already incarcerated there and affiliated with a white supremacist gang in the prison, and they took Keith as a soldier in exchange for protection. All of one hundred thirty pounds, Keith was sure to face abuse on his own.

On the day he was released, Keith went to go see his grandmother, probably his favourite person in the world. In addition to standard grandmotherly spoiling when he was young, she had provided a place to run away from home to, or bail money when his parents refused it. When Keith was in prison she arranged for him to visit her in the hospital on more than one occasion so her son could slip him an ounce of hash, which Keith took back to the prison in his rectum.

True to form, Grandma had a few special things planned for her grandson on the day of his release from prison for armed robbery: a stocked bar, some more hash, five hundred dollars in spending money, even a prostitute. Keith thought it was everything he could want. It would turn out to be more than he bargained for.

That night, the prostitute introduced him to freebase cocaine, more widely known today as crack cocaine. Keith had managed to shake off his heroin addiction in prison, only to have a new monkey jump on his back immediately upon his return to freedom. A few months later, fiending and in need of cash, Keith snuck into his grandmother's house in the middle of the night. He crept up to her bed while she slept, put a pillow over her face and began taping her up. He gagged her, threw her into a chair, pushed the chair into the closet and closed the doors so he wouldn't have to hear her cries. Keith proceeded to ransack the house and take all of the money before fleeing to go score.

Unsurprisingly, Keith forgot about his grandmother in the haze of drugs, and it was only when her son came over three days later that she was rescued, still bound and gagged in the closet, dehydrated and soiled.

For this deed, Keith became estranged from his family, not that he had been particularly close with them in adulthood. For her part, his grandmother said she couldn't forgive him yet, but she would one day when he quit drugs for good.

According to Keith, he ended up in Winnipeg for a while around this time, drifting through the same haze of drugs, crime and violence. The dates become unclear here: Keith says in 1992 he left the city with a bang, robbing a large restaurant/bar in The Forks tourist district one night before boarding a bus to Vancouver with his accomplices. He says he personally walked out with thirty-seven thousand dollars in cash, including an envelope five inches thick with hundred-dollar bills. They were never caught.

The tale is problematic. The bar in question, which is now closed, did not open until 1995, and I could find neither a contemporary news item nor a police report. These things don't necessarily disqualify the story: The dates could be a slip of faded memory; not all robberies are reported in the press, as an acquaintance at the *Winnipeg Free Press* pointed out; and the alleged incident took place so long ago that it's entirely reasonable that it may not be in the Winnipeg Police computer database, said the kind officer who checked for me.

It is certainly possible that the story happened exactly as Keith tells it, or it could be complete bullshit, or somewhere on the spectrum between those two. Personally, given the context of our interview where Keith seemed genuinely interested in being forthcoming and straightforward with his life story, I lean toward believing that the story is broadly true, though perhaps exaggerated or mistaken through errors of memory. But the story remains unconfirmed, and as a journalist, I have to be unsatisfied with it.

The next part, though, rings true: while in Calgary for a brief stop en route to Vancouver, Keith and his partners in crime went to the bar and had a few. When the time came to reboard the bus, they were refused on the grounds of alcohol consumption. "I had thirty-seven thousand dollars in cash in my pocket and a nine-millimetre gun. I didn't give a fuck. See ya. I walked out and been stuck here since."

Keith and his friends left the station and got a motel room. He kept his handgun tucked into the back of his pants when he went to get ice to keep their beer cold. It was then that he encountered a girl and a guy in the hallway who were arguing. Keith thought she was attractive—"a hot little number ... I was thinking of getting a blow job at the time"—and decided to step in and be the tough guy. He told the guy to beat it: "Why don't you fucking bounce before you end up getting fucked up?" is his rough recollection of the phrasing. The guy didn't argue; he just slinked away. The girl introduced herself as Cristy.

"[She] told me after, 'We seen that gun. Like, who the fuck are you? Cop?'" He assured her he was not, and his fantasy came true: they became lovers, even moving in together.

Things fell apart nine months later when they were swarmed by police while walking downtown. They were told to get on the ground immediately, and Keith knew it was about the Winnipeg robbery. "Something I gotta tell you, baby."

Except they weren't there for him; Cristy was the one being arrested. Keith shut his mouth. They cuffed her and took her away, and then a cop began asking him questions.

> He tells me, "Do you know who this is?" I said, "Yeah, her name's [Cristy]." He goes, "No, her name's fucking [Megan]." I'm like, "Buddy, you don't know what the fuck you're talking about. I'm pounding that pussy, I know her name." He goes, "Are you sure you want to say that?" I'm like, "Yeah, buddy." But again, I'm thinking her name is [Cristy], her ID says [Cristy], and she's twenty years old. Well she's actually fucking sixteen years old, her name's [Megan] and she's an escapee out of the youth detention centre. I'm borderline getting charged with a statutory rape charge now.

This seems like the conclusion of a side story, but few things are so simple in Keith's narrative. Megan went back to jail for a year and a half, and when she was released she reconciled with her family, moved in with Keith again and became pregnant. Their relationship would last about six years, up until the day she gave birth to their second child. Keith's recollection of what happened is as follows, though it's worth remembering that his ability to clearly perceive the situation at the time was clouded by addictions.

> We had broken up, and then she found out that she was pregnant. She come back, and we decided we're going to work on things. But what she had neglected to tell me was, she had sold the kid for expenses, medical expenses. She already made agreements with her aunty, and her aunty was paying her money and I knew nothing of this until the day he was born. To this day, I've never, ever seen that boy. I don't know what colour hair he has, what colour skin he has, whether he's my boy. She told me in the hospital, just before going into the delivery room, that he wouldn't be coming home. She had actually made plans with her aunty. And upon her telling me that, I spit in her face, fucking [he chuckles here] shoved the doctor that was in there out of my way and walked out, never went back.

These are the types of stories his life is filled with: grotesque twists on a bumpy road that never seems to get much sunlight.

\* \* \*

Movers love stories. We love to recount grand and terrible tales of jobs past, often spicing them up with mild or outrageous exaggerations. They are our fishing stories: the heaviest pieces are always heavier in the telling than in the carrying; likewise for the longest days, and kindest and meanest customers. Bragging and out-doing each other is a very human trait, but often we simply want to share something crazy or impressive with someone who understands.

Perhaps moving lends itself to outrageous stories more than

most jobs. After all, every day is different, improvisational problem solving is often needed and we are dealing with exceptionally heavy, large and expensive objects. If a box spring or couch won't fit in the stairwell, we'll hoist it up to the second floor with straps. We'll try anything before we admit defeat, a trait that produces some impressive and endlessly exaggerated tales.

Of course, not all stories are told with pride.

There's the time Jesse, while working for another company years ago, let his unlicensed partner drive the moving truck back after a job. It was the middle of the night and Jesse felt he was too exhausted to safely drive back into the city. His partner insisted he could do it, and Jesse agreed. He fell asleep at the wheel on the highway and crashed the truck, flipping it on its side.

There's the time a guy at another company got a five-ton truck wedged on the lower deck of the Centre Street Bridge, an absurd place to consider driving a truck given that it has a 2.3 metre clearance.

My personal all-time favourite moving story might be one that Darwin tells from his early days in Regina. He'd been booked for a move, but the customer was unable to meet him at the load-up, so she gave him the address and said she'd leave the door unlocked. Darwin and his worker arrived, loaded the truck and drove to the new address, where they found the customer waiting, as planned. They began bringing furniture into the house. After a few items, the customer noticed something was wrong. *Where did you get that? And that? Wait, this isn't my stuff!*

They'd gone to the wrong address—which just happened to be unlocked with no one home—and cleaned it out from top to bottom. Darwin drove back as fast as he could and, finding no one there, quickly replaced the furniture and left, the inhabitants never the wiser. Unintentional robbery. Accidental larceny.

Another tale that has taken its place in the mythology of Darwin's Moving is the move of the boss's mother. Darwin agreed to come move her within Winnipeg after the local moving company she originally hired charged her an exorbitant amount of money for the first phase of the job. The plan was to drive out from Calgary in his pickup truck with Gavin and Jesse and rent a moving truck in Winnipeg. But, true to form, Gavin and Jesse got blackout drunk the night before and failed to turn up at the yard. Furious, Darwin hit the road on his own.

They came to and called the boss with apologies. (Jesse, predictably, also tried to argue that Darwin should have waited for them.) With his usual abundance of forgiveness, Darwin paid for them to fly to Winnipeg, a kindness also likely due to the fact that he preferred working with guys he knew rather than random day-hires and wanted his friends with him for what was sure to be a stressful job.

Darwin's mom was moving out of a large-ish, run-of-the-mill suburban home. The first moving company had taken a sizable load away, but there was still a great deal left in the house, much of it loose items like shoes and clothes that needed to be packed. The three of them worked from early each morning until late each night, when Gavin and Jesse would go back to their cheap motel and get drunk before passing out for a short sleep. It was an exhausting and endless job. After five days of work, they were glad to head back to Calgary.

Some stories are based around superlatives: the heaviest piece, the longest job, the biggest tip. My heaviest piece was an authentic red British telephone booth. Made of cast iron, it weighed 1,900 pounds and required six strong men just to slide it down the truck ramp. (Several hot tubs have also come close to that mark, though with the extra challenge of lifting them over a backyard fence.)

I don't recall any specific longest day, but there have been a few that touched the twenty-hour mark. There're a few entries in my worst-customer column. But there's a clear winner for my worst fuck-up.

We break things. It's inevitable. There is no such thing as a perfect mover. No matter how careful, no matter how experienced, given enough jobs over enough time you will break something.

Most damages are due to carelessness, rushing or inexperience. Movers get tired, or overconfident, and something dings a wall, or a table scratches a new hardwood floor. Not everything breaks while being carried. A poor pack job in the truck can have disastrous results: metal snaps, wood scratches, glass cracks.

When damage occurs, the mood of the move darkens. The depth of the shadow is directly proportional to the severity of the accident. Most movers, or at least those who take pride in their job, absolutely hate when something breaks. They are ashamed of it. The best movers take it personally. Jesse chatters constantly on a job, but if something breaks he won't say a word for twenty minutes. Even those movers less invested in the work curse themselves when they damage something because of the inevitable consequence: the customer must be informed. Part of the horror lore people create around moving companies stems from their propensity for damaging homes and furniture, sometimes shamelessly covering it up. Everyone fears their movers will break something. We truly hate validating those fears. Which brings me to the worst fuck-up of my entire moving career.

It's the final piece of the day, made all the more enticing in the cold darkness of late November 2014. It's only been half a day, only the load-up. Tomorrow we'll unload. I'm working with Geoffrey, the affable sixty-one-year-old Brit, more full of jokes and charm than great strength or moving prowess. Geoffrey has some careless tendencies when carrying a piece, bumping into walls or grazing doors a little too often, even if damage does not always result.

But today has gone well, a fairly pleasant five-hour gig begun at noon. Geoffrey is great company and we're still cracking jokes and bantering as we tackle the final piece of the day.

The Big Green Egg, a specialty ceramic barbecue brand so named for its shape and colour, comes in many sizes and varieties. This one is approximately two and a half feet in diameter and weighs maybe three hundred pounds. The enamel exterior is smooth and slick, save for a hinge that forms a natural handle. The egg is seated on a metal stand below a circular cut-out in a wooden table. The only way to move it is to lift the egg straight up. Since there is no space for hands to fit between egg and table, we slide a strap below it. With Geoffrey and me on either side of the strap, and the customer Colin close by, the egg rises unsteadily. Geoffrey can lift it, but he struggles to raise it high enough to clear the table, and the egg wobbles severely and winds up on its side on the table. It wasn't pretty, but it's free.

We've pulled the truck around to the back alley. The path to it involves three steps down from the deck, and then a straight shot through the garage and out. As we try to tip the precarious thing upright on the table, it disobeys and somehow bashes our customer in the forehead.

He says he's okay, so we turn our attention back to the task at hand. I suggest tipping the egg back to Geoffrey so he can carry from the hinge handle and I from the bottom. Colin suggests that the hinge isn't made for carrying. I wave this off, telling him I've carried several of these barbecues before just like this without any mishaps. The hinge protrudes nearly two inches, made of heavy black metal with a space for a hand to grip. With a smooth body devoid of any other protrusions or edges, this is the perfect and obvious handle. Why else would they have designed it as such?

It's heavy and awkward but we lug it down the stairs toward the garage. I'm bending low as I walk backwards, since we can't tip it too far back lest the lid open.

"Are you okay?" asks Geoffrey in his handsome British accent.

"I was born good, I only got better," I reply, and we laugh as we reach the side door of the truck. We've elected not to set up the ramp, since we have only the barbecue and a propane space heater to load. The heater was no problem to lift up into the truck from the ground. Now we raise the tilted barbecue. Geoffrey—older and shorter than me, lacking the reserves of strength to ignore tired muscles—struggles as he lifts awkwardly from the handle.

It happens in an instant. In the darkness, I'm not even sure what has happened. The barbecue falls away from me out of my hands, and my first thought is that Geoffrey has dropped his side. It happens so fast that there is no hope of saving it. Down. Smash. Smashed like a hollow egg, like a Fabergé or pysanka, the only colours here being dark green paint and the creamy white of the violently exposed ceramic.

I don't know what Geoffrey and Colin were thinking or feeling at that moment. I was barely aware of their presence. Forceful emotions and thoughts were screaming through my mind.

Failure.

Embarrassment.

Anger.

So stupid.

You're so stupid.

This is your fault.

Expensive.

Those things cost a fortune.

Failure.

Darwin.

God

fucking

damn it.

I turn to Colin. I say something stupid in a misguided attempt at humour, something like, "Well, I guess we don't have to move it now!" I immediately reassure him that we—Darwin—will take care of it. The barbecue is clearly beyond repair, shattered into a thousand pieces. All that remains intact are the metal parts, which we collect and deposit in the back of the customer's pickup. Many sincere apologies later, Geoffrey and I confirm the time and address for the unload tomorrow and say good night. We climb into the truck. Geoffrey is driving, as his car was at the yard and I will jump out near Crowchild Trail.

I was furious with myself. I am the one responsible for the move. There are big moments of embarrassment so awful that they cling to us for the duration of our lives. Perhaps you wet your pants in an elementary school class, or scored on your own goal in a basketball game as the crowd laughed. These are things that stay with you. For the rest of my life I will remember how I felt as that green egg fell, in slow motion, to the icy ground.

I call Darwin as Geoffrey drives and give him the news. He takes it as just another setback, just another piece of shit on his ever-growing pile. He figures it'll set him back about seven hundred dollars. I apologize profusely, but his tone doesn't change from weary defeat. I hang up and jump out before Geoffrey turns onto Crowchild.

As I walk home, I call Darwin again.

"Hey man, I didn't want to say this in front of Geoffrey, but if you want to not pay me for today, I don't mind. In fact, it'd make me feel better."

"Well, I appreciate that, but it's fine. You said you were carrying it and it was an accident, so that's just doing your job. That happens. If you were fucking around, that would be different. But I'm not going to punish you for just doing your job."

I apologize again and hang up. The warm shower and cold beer waiting for me at home are welcome respites. Then my phone rings. It's Darwin, sounding more animated.

"Hey man, I just wanted to tell you about Keithy." Apparently, Keith had been scheduled to work that morning at ten thirty but failed to show. He'd just called Darwin now, at night, saying that he'd slept in and rushed to the yard but found no one there:

he must have just missed them. Darwin listened to this excuse but didn't tell Keith that he was at the yard until three. He'd caught Keith in a blatant lie and couldn't resist telling someone.

"These guys, man, they all just lie. They lie and lie and lie and they think I'm stupid." He laughs. "Anyway. I'll talk to you later."

It was a short call. All he'd wanted was a friend to talk to. I was still that friend. I felt better after that.

\* \* \*

When I went into work the following week, taped to the inside of the warehouse door was an invoice from a barbecue shop for one large Big Green Egg, plus assembly and delivery costs. The total was $1,420.

Written in large letters with black marker underneath:

Please: Do Not use the handles to lift this BBQ!!

\* \* \*

After his relationship ended with delivery-day drama, Keith fell deeper into drugs, especially crack and crystal meth. For the next three years he stayed at the Salvation Army's Booth Centre, a large homeless shelter in Calgary's rough Downtown East Village neighbourhood. Employment hauling construction fences and as a furniture mover for a well-known van line provided the money for his habit.

This was not a good time in his life. Keith the Addict was also Keith the Dealer, Keith the Robber, Keith the Violent and Unpredictable.

He tells me a story about a time he was smoking crack just south of downtown, where Macleod Trail crosses the Elbow River.

I was doing a big blast. Buddy came walking towards

me. I never used to hide when I was on the dope, I did it, I didn't care. He was like, Hey, got any more of that? Like, yeah, maybe. How do I know you even smoke dope (and) you're not a cop or nothing? And he wanted an ounce. So I charged him eleven hundred dollars for the ounce. But I had to make sure he smoked it first. So I took him under the bridge that's there on Macleod. And did a blast in the pipe, glass stem pipe, and then I put one in for him. He was sitting on the rocks and I was standing in front of him. And as he proceeded to put that pipe to his lips and heat it, I kicked him in the face with a steel-toe boot on, causing the pipe to shatter over his face, and making him smash his head on the rocks and knocking him out. I took his eleven hundred dollars and as I'm leaving, cutting through the parking lot of the casino, I found a wallet ... that had twelve hundred dollars in it! I kid you not. So I went back to the Sally Ann where I was staying, in the Booth Centre there, third floor, and I stayed in there for a week. I didn't come out because I was scared every boogeyman was out there, I was so high and fucked up from smoking dope. I smoked dope for a week straight in my room.

Sadly, this tale is not an aberration or anomaly. This was normal life, and there are many more stories of bad deeds, some involving Keith's "brother". For the sake of preventing the identification of anyone involved, I have changed some personal details and will say as little as possible about this man—only that he is not Keith's real brother, he does not live in Calgary and he is involved in a white supremacist organization. Many people in Keith's life would fit this vague description, including the man I will call Joe.

What happened was me and my brother had come to town to grab an ounce [of crack] for him and his wife and me for back home. We were staying in Hanna at the time. Anyways, off we go. Me and him ended up smoking all the dope. We had no money. We were scared to go home because his wife's going to lose it on us. So we have to find somebody to rob. So I said, Well I know these black guys that are selling. Let's set 'em up. So I phoned them up, and the black guy is a little nervous because we'd never put in such a large order. So he come over, brought the dope up to me, and my brother was playing the part as the driver. And he's playing the part that he's scared to get out because there's a half dozen black guys standing around. And we're going to pick up an ounce of dope off them. So I convinced the one guy he could keep the dope on him, but he had to come to the vehicle with me. And he convinces his buddies that they're going to stay behind.

Well, we got over to the vehicle and my brother took a gun up beside the door, high enough so the guy could see it through the window. And demanded the dope. Buddy just passed him the dope, he didn't want to get shot at the moment. So he gave him the fucking dope, I jumped in the truck, and the nigger turned around and started screaming at his buddies, and I'm glad it was a stolen Suburban 'cause all the windows were blown out of it. We fucked off, they were chasing us, shooting at us, trying to stop us. We were just running down, smashing into cars along 14th [Street SW] there, just having a great old time, smoking dope, and got away. We got away.

It was during this time that Keith met a couple I'll call Jack and Lucy. They were drug customers of his, and they eventually asked him to move in with them to make their rent more affordable. Keith agreed. Shortly thereafter he met T-Bone—"Probably weighed about 340 pounds, about five foot ten inches, big fat black boy"—who showed him how to make extremely cheap imitation crack cocaine from over-the-counter items, including household chemicals. "Of course you wouldn't get high. But it would smoke, it sounded and looked and tasted like crack cocaine. I had people begging me for it, and there was zero cocaine in it."

It cost him about five dollars per pound to manufacture the fake stuff. Considering that a pound of real crack in Canada sells for anywhere between twenty thousand and sixty thousand dollars, depending on the quality and other factors, Keith had found a very lucrative way to take advantage of his fellow addicts. The money was more than enough to support his rent and his (authentic) crack habit, and he stopped working his other jobs.

Meanwhile, Jack had thrown Lucy out of the house. Lucy was a bipolar schizophrenic drug user, a volatile situation for someone surrounded by unstable addicts. Then Jack was arrested for drug trafficking. (In Keith's improbable telling of it, he, Jack and another friend were sitting and drinking in the house one night when Jack went outside to find the police there ready to arrest him for drug trafficking. Satisfied that they'd gotten their man, the cops left without approaching the house. This happened unbeknownst to the men inside, who wondered what had happened to their friend.).

Keith got another roommate and continued his usual activities. One day, Lucy called. She'd heard Jack was in jail and wondered if she could move back in. Keith agreed.

So she came back to live with me, and because I'd already moved [a new roommate] in, she lived in my bedroom and I lived out in the living room. I gave her a private room because she was a female, a little safety spot. Well, from that it went to, a month and a month later ... of course she's a cute little thing, young little blonde ... I'm a guy, I'm trying to get into her fucking pants, get a little bit of pussy. And she says, If you stop selling dope and go back to work, you could have a little bit of this pussy.

So Keith went back to legitimate work, and they became lovers. Lucy was in her mid-twenties, nearly two decades his junior. He says she told him that she was medically unable to conceive, and so they didn't use protection. It wasn't long before Lucy was pregnant.

* * *

Hey, baby. Yeah, just going to unload. I dunno, probably another four hours of work. Did you go downtown? Why didn't you go downtown, baby? What did you get at Walmart? Did you get food? What did you get? Nice. Nice. What else did you get? Did you get cigarettes? Did you get that other thing, the green thing? Nice. How much did it all cost? What's left? Well if you still got money, you get the fuck back out there and spend it, woman! I'm just kidding, baby. Thank you for going out. Yeah. Yeah, me and Staś, Snuggles, he's driving us over to unload now. Hey, you know what'd be really nice? What I'd really like? Some beer. It's been a while since you let me have any beer. Do you want to go get me some? Just like a fifteen-pack of Brewhouse, that place on the corner. Yeah, when you go out. Thanks, baby. Yeah, that'd be nice. What's that? Heh, what's that? Your ass is hurting from last night? Ha! Don't worry baby, when I get home I'll straighten out that ass for you. Don't you worry, baby. Heh. Okay. See you soon, baby. I love you.

* * *

Cochrane is a small town a short drive past the northwest border of Calgary. Its charming old streets and genuine Western ranching community feel are still there today, though they have been diluted by folks who have come to use their prosperity to build a suburban utopia without the meddlesome pushers of density and transit: big, flashy homes, expensive vehicles, sprawling parking lots surrounding big-box chain retailers.

But my favourite part of Cochrane still hasn't changed: the approach to the valley in which it lies. The route from the north pitches down sharply as the road curves along the front of the Big Hill that looms above the town. The view from here as the valley suddenly opens up to reveal a beautiful panorama of rolling foothills leading to muscular peaks is nothing short of breathtaking, no matter how many times you have experienced it.

It's late April and I'm working with Keith. It's not supposed to be a big job, from a townhouse on the north side to a house in a new development on the south side. The weather is nice, the Flames have a home playoff game in a few hours and we are in good moods.

I steer the white truck to the job. We find cars blocking the driveway so I park the truck just up the narrow street for the time being, and we go inside to have a look.

Our customers are nice people, a well-organized couple who are quite prepared for their move. Keith and I take a walk through the house, examining the job. There's not much disassembling required, and much of the furniture is cheap and light.

We put our shoes back on and head back outside. As I walk toward the truck I turn to look at the house, checking the height of the second-storey balcony for truck clearance. Then I am falling. I've taken only two or three steps backwards, but the driveway is shorter than usual and I am closer to the rolled curb at the end of it than I realize. Before my brain can compute what is happening, some low-level process or instinct automatically extends my hand backwards.

There are eight bones in the human wrist, roughly divided into two rows. One of them, the scaphoid, is shaped like a big cashew and sits on the thumb side of the arrangement. This is the bone that broke when my palm collided with the pavement with my full body weight behind it.

Keith's voice, rough and concerned: "You okay, Staś?" I quickly scramble to my feet as I realize the customer is outside with us. He'd just watched me fall down like an idiot. Under ordinary circumstances I might feel a bit sheepish. As a paid professional about to carry and transport all of this man's personal belongings, I am mortified.

The customer asks if I'm all right and I laugh it off, dust my hand and butt, make a couple jokes at my own expense. Both he and Keith seem genuinely concerned. You landed pretty hard, they tell me. I assure them I am fine. I back the truck into the driveway and we begin the job.

My wrist hurts, but not particularly bad at first. I figure it's a mild sprain. As the load progresses and I carry boxes and furniture to the truck, the pain begins to increase. I use packing tape as a wrap to compress and strengthen the joint, but by the end of the load-up the pain is unignorable.

The move takes about six hours. By the end, I am unable to lift much and Keith takes care of the boxes. Once he knows I'm in pain, he insists I not strain the injury further. Fortunately most of the furniture is light enough that I can struggle through the job without fear of dropping something. Everything goes well and the customers seem happy. No tip.

I manage to drive the truck back to Calgary with some difficulty, shifting gears gingerly with the damaged hand. Keith leaves on his bicycle and I walk to the bus stop. I still don't think the wrist is broken. I go home, shower, invite my father over to watch the Flames' playoff game while icing the wrist and feeding it beer. The Flames win, and we walk down to the Red Mile for a taste of the celebration. But I have to admit that the pain is ruining my enjoyment of the moment, so we leave and I go home to bed. The throbbing pain chases sleep from me, and in the morning the swelling is still so severe and unchanged that I decide to have it checked out.

The x-ray shows the break and I'll wear a full forearm cast for the next ten weeks. After that comes months of physiotherapy. Though my summer fun is limited, workers' compensation comes through and I get my regular wages. But Darwin loses the one guy he could always count on, his only regular driver, right at the start of the busy season.

* * *

Keith and Lucy's son was born to parents who no doubt loved him but were handicapped in their ability to care for him. Drug addiction, mental illness and poverty meant that they had difficulty managing their own lives, let alone adequately caring for a young, dependent child. Keith, for one, had never really had anyone who could be called a good parental figure in his life. Childcare is far more than simply providing food and shelter and physical safety. Could someone like Keith be a father in the most meaningful sense of the word?

Over the five years since the boy's birth, there have been many ups and downs, to say the least. I won't plumb the depths of this period, partly out of consideration for the family and their privacy, partly because it would amount largely to tilling the same fields we have visited elsewhere in these pages. Suffice to say that if the covering cloth is left in place, a reasonable reader would not do badly guessing the shape of things underneath.

Keith loves his son a great deal. I have seen tears in his eyes when he talks about him, about how they might take him away from him yet again, cutting off his visitation rights. He insists that his love for his son is the one thing with the potential to keep him on the straight and narrow.

How much is a parent's love worth? What price should a child have to pay for it? Is a mediocre father who makes questionable choices but fills his child with love and self-worth better than a responsible man who is emotionally distant and often absent? Where does the balance lie between imperfect parenting and a dangerous situation? At what point is it worth the risk of throwing the child into the system and hoping for the best? There is more grey area here than we might want to admit, and social agencies without appropriate resources struggle to make these high-stakes judgement calls every day.

The idea that Keith's love for his son could help him save his own life is an appealing one. But it's worth noting how frighteningly easy it is for him to slide back into his darker persona.

Lucy left Keith for the first time when their son was two years old. Keith's "brother" had shown up at the door covered in blood. Lucy called Keith to inform him, and when he got home she was gone. It was just him and Joe.

The blood belonged to the man in the car. The car also belonged to the man in the car, though Joe was in possession of both. Joe had needed a ride when he arrived to town, so he asked a man in a car for a light. When the man rolled down the window, Joe hit him, hauled him out, beat him and put him in the trunk before driving away in broad daylight. When Keith got home, the man was still in the car, which is to say he was in the trunk.

They abandoned the stolen car. The man in the trunk was black, which seems unlikely to be a coincidence given that Joe was a white supremacist.

We ended up just dumping him, leaving him. Walking away from the car, leaving him in the car. And we walked away. Whether he lived or not, I'll never know. I don't know. We dumped the car and he was in it.

There followed a period of drugs, crime and violence, the very things that Keith wanted to leave behind him. But he couldn't resist with Joe around. It was too easy, too familiar, too comfortable. And Joe was not a man about to take a negative answer from anyone, not even his brother.

A couple weeks later the boys stole another car en route to a white supremacist New Year's party. The evening eventually led to another kidnapping of a black man. They had smoked his dope and when he was unable to get them more, "he became the dope," as Keith puts it. Back at Keith's place, they tied him to a chair and beat the hell out of him.

Then Keith made an unlikely choice. When his brother took a break to use the washroom, he cut the rope and freed the man.

'Cause I knew he was going to end up in a BFI bin. Slowly beaten to death. My brother was in that state of mind. [...] And I didn't want any part of that. And I knew if I let him go, I was gonna have a beating. But I'm not gonna die. I'm just going to have a beating and my brother's going to spit on me and tell me how much he hates me. But he's gonna get over it. [...]

I think it has something to do with the fact that we were in my house, my son had been there, we had ran out of dope, my brain was starting to click back in. I could see my son's stuff. And I was asking myself, What the fuck am I doing? Why am I doing this again? And I think for a second I grew a conscience. And also, I did know him. I'd known him for a long time, this guy. So did my brother. And that's why he felt safe coming with us. And it was a mistake for him to even come with us. I knew what was going to happen. My brother knew what was going to happen. We just took advantage of the guy, and when we ran out of dope, we did what we had to. We beat him and beat him and beat him. And as we were sobering up, I think I grew a bit of a conscience for a minute, because my brother went to the bathroom and when he came out he was gone. And then me and my brother got into it. He gave me a little bit of a licking. And two days later my brother left.

As dark and awful as this story is—and it truly is—there is something remarkable here. Keith chose to spare an innocent man knowing full well he was also choosing to suffer in his place. It was a moment of clarity for a violent, troubled addict. Keith describes it as growing a conscience, but I like to think that in that moment, when the drugs had lessened their hold on him, he was able to be himself—the kind, self-deprecating person I know and customers love, the person he was never really given a chance to be.

\* \* \*

Winding slowly through the narrow streets of a villa-style development on the outskirts of the city, I search for the truck. Most of the houses are still under construction, and I have to navigate around workers and equipment while looking up and down each street. Finally I spot a big familiar rectangle on wheels parked outside a house.

I pull up behind the blue truck and walk over to the ramp. No one is around. Inside I see Jesse folding a pad, his back to me.

"Hey, beautiful. You're doing that wrong."

He turns and smiles. "Hey, bud." He extends his hand down to me and we shake, then grip. "How's it goin'?"

I hop up into the truck and we catch up quickly. He asks about my wrist, and about the book. I tell him both are close but not quite ready. It's been a long summer of healing and physiotherapy just to get me back to this point, my first move since that day in Cochrane when I broke my wrist. Today I'm the extra guy on the job, here to unload for a couple hours only, nothing heavier than a hundred pounds or so.

Keith comes into the truck. "Holy shit, you're still alive!" I say in jest. Ricky Roy follows behind him. "Holy shit, *you're* still alive!" We all laugh. Ricky sports a beard and a dull expression. Keith has grown hair and looks significantly older than a few months ago, before his disappearance.

The truck is already a third emptied. I grab a chair and head inside, where I find Darwin and our customers.

While walking from the basement back to the truck, I remind Keith that I need to talk to him to finish the book. After a series of interviews, usually while driving to and from jobs, we were only halfway through his life story when Keith disappeared for two months. His addictions had pulled him back into the darkness. Now he's back working, but he tells me his life has been chaos. He's homeless at the moment, sleeping in a tent in the Foothills industrial district. But he's moving into a place after the weekend, and his life will calm down then, and he promises to finish the interview.

After an hour, the unload is finished and the boys head back to get the second load while Darwin and I stay behind. We work through the pile of pads on the driveway, pulling packing tape off and folding them into neat stacks.

The boss is stressed. During the unload he discovered the truck engine is leaking antifreeze, which could mean the engine—which he installed five or six years ago—is shot, or at least not worth fixing.

"I figured that engine—cost me thirteen thousand dollars—

I figured it would be good for the life of that truck," he says with dismay in his voice. "It's Jesse and his crazy driving. He doesn't care. He doesn't get it. He's going to drive that truck into the ground."

We catch up on our lives, with long stretches of unawkward silence in between conversation. The sound of tape separating from pads and pads being shaken competes in our ears with the dusty wind. It's been months since we did this together, and it's familiar and comfortable.

Darwin and I assemble and shift some furniture inside the house at the customer's behest. She leaves to answer the phone as we finish putting together a bed.

"You know," says the boss, "I like moving. I do. I always have other things I have to do, but I like doing this. It relaxes me."

"Well, yeah," I reply, "of course it does. Because you're in control."

"What do you mean?"

"All the things in your life that give you stress—guys not showing up for work, stuff breaking, the truck engine giving out—is all stuff you can't control. When you're on the job, moving furniture, you're in control."

Darwin's eyes lower as he considers this for a few moments. "Huh. I never thought of it like that." He purses his lips and then gives a sharp nod. "That's pretty good, Lambertski."

We laugh as we walk back upstairs.

* * *

On the twelfth floor of the Calgary Courts Centre, Keith and Lucy are waiting for their case to be heard. It's a child welfare hearing to determine whether their five-year-old son, who is already in the custody of Lucy's mother, should stay there permanently.

I'm here because I've been stalking Keith for weeks, still unable to nail him down to finish interviewing him. We make plans to meet, but he always cancels or disappears at the last minute. Darwin knows this routine well, and the usual tired excuses afterwards. But when Keith doesn't show up for work, the job must still get done. Darwin calls someone else. I have no one else to call. I can't finish my book without Keith's co-operation. He told me to meet him at court today because it was an appointment he couldn't break, and his day afterwards was wide open. Finally, I will have my interview.

The judge enters, tells everyone to sit, and Keith's case is called. He and Lucy approach the defence table, but the social worker accompanying them tells Keith to sit at the table behind them.

The judge skims the file before addressing the parents. He asks if this is what they want to do. Lucy says yes. The judge asks what the father thinks, and Keith stands and says it's best for the boy and he has no choice. Well, no, you do have a choice, is the reply from the bench. The judge asks if they understand what a permanent custody order means—that they will never have a claim to get their kid back, and that there's no guarantee that he'll live with his grandmother forever. This is the point of no return.

Lucy talks about how she's doing better with the things she needs to do. She's not there yet, but she believes she can get there one day. Hang on, says the judge, if you think you can get to a place where you can care for your child, why are you agreeing to permanently give him up?

Keith is still standing, hands jammed in his pockets, slightly swaying uncomfortably. His body language is defensive. We don't have no choice, he says roughly. Have you spoken to a lawyer to discuss your options? asks the judge. Buddy, I can't afford five hundred buck an hour for no lawyer. [He says "buck," singular, perhaps a tic of speech due to his nerves.]

There's legal aid, there's options to understand the situation before you. The judge looks at the file. There's a deadline of December

6 on this application, so we have lots of time before a decision needs to be made. Based on what you've told me, I'm not sure you're ready to agree to this very serious and permanent decision.

As the judge speaks, Keith suddenly turns and walks back to the audience gallery. Lucy's mother is sitting there and he asks her what she thinks. I can't hear their discussion. He saunters back up to address the judge.

I'm good, he says. It's what's best for the boy and I don't have no choice.

You do have a choice, Mr. _____, says the judge. I wonder if Keith has ever been addressed like that by someone other than a judge or official.

There's some more back and forth on the idea of choice and seeking legal advice. Keith stands and rocks, addressing the judge with sharpness in his voice. He feels threatened. The judge is actually very kind and polite. Keith doesn't understand that he's trying to help them. The judge sees they feel boxed in by the system and he wants to stop them from making a rash, irreversible decision against their will. But to Keith, he's just another guy causing him fucking problems.

The case is put off until the end of the month. I leave the courtroom and stand outside, giving space to the family. Keith knows I'm there, knows he's coming with me afterwards. We take the elevator down, and Keith, Lucy and her mother talk quietly together in the lobby.

Suddenly Lucy starts shouting. I did what you wanted, I was gonna do it, so fuck you! Calm down, baby, calm down, Keith says softly. Lucy storms off. Keith walks quickly after her, and I after him. We pass a sheriff as we approach the exit gates.

Keith is a walking visual stereotype. When he briskly follows a young, upset woman out of a courthouse, people will pay attention. The sheriff turns and follows me. As we pass through the exit gates into the outer lobby, there is a large window that provides a clear view to the street. Lucy is visibly upset. Keith restrains her from leaving. In doing so, he shoves her. Not terribly hard—she takes only one step backward as a result—but it doesn't matter. The sheriff rushes ahead of me, already calling for backup on his radio.

*Hands against the wall, buddy.*

*I didn't do nothing.*

*HANDS AGAINST THE WALL!*

*She's my fucking wife!* Keith protests as the hands of the law are roughly laid upon him and he's pressed face-first into the wall. He knows better than to struggle. Two more sheriffs are on the scene. They handcuff him and lead him back inside.

*Lucy! Lucy, gimme twenty bucks, I'm going to jail!*

As Keith gets swallowed back into the palace of justice I call to the young sheriff who initially followed me out. I explain that I'm a friend of the man they just arrested, as well a journalist writing a book about him. I ask when he might be released.

He looks at me in my dress coat and collared shirt for a moment and answers in the same polite manner in which I addressed him. He says they'll hold him for a while, but he doesn't know how long. I can see what he is thinking: why the hell would you write a book about *this* guy?

I thank him and walk down the street with two thoughts. First: if it had been someone who looked like me in Keith's shoes, would the scenario have played out differently? Second: I'm never going to get this goddamn interview.

\* \* \*

I have thus far avoided any temptation to wax political in these pages. This book is meant to be merely a series of portraits, and the reader's own politics will inform his or her view of things. But allow me to make one point that I feel is worth considering.

While all empirical evidence demonstrates that rehabilitation of criminals is far more effective than tough punishment by any metric—from financial cost of the system, to overall crime rate, the likelihood of re-offending and so on—there are always those who advocate for harsher treatment of those on the fringes of civil society.

But even the toughest law-and-order right-wingers this side of Afghanistan must agree that rehabilitation, where possible (a crucial and debatable point), is beneficial to society. If the main argument against rehabilitation as public policy is that it doesn't work, then in the cases when it does work it must surely be a good thing.

In Canada, we broadly acknowledge this argument in our approach to justice—more than the United States, less than, say, Sweden. The laws and approaches change with the government of the day, but as a nation we ostensibly subscribe to the idea that it is generally better and more effective to help a troubled person than simply give him or her a timeout.

I would argue that Keith is the very definition of a person our system is supposed to help but didn't. All of his most serious crimes were committed during times when he was desperately addicted to powerful street drugs. His drug use directly stems from the abuse he suffered as a child. From everything he's told me, it seems fair to draw the conclusion that his family was more of a corrupting influence than a safe haven.

More than that, Keith *wants* to be better. He rejected his family's racist ideology. (The racial slurs that crop up in his speech occasionally are habitual vestiges from his bad old days—certainly not acceptable or excusable, but also not sincere.) He fears his brother's influence and avoids him. He wants to be a father to his son, even though he has no idea how. He wants to be a decent person, but he's never been anything other than what he is. How much of that was his choice?

Keith is a violent criminal and depraved addict, but he is also a good man. With customers, he is friendly and self-deprecating, even goofy, and they love him for it. On a job he works as hard as Jesse and will do anything to please the customer. He regularly displays kindness and generosity: *Hey Staś, want half my sandwich? Hey Snuggles, customer gave me this computer monitor, you want it?*

The people who argue for tough jail terms over rehabilitation are often the same ones sounding the chorus of choice: they chose this life, they chose to break the law, they chose to do drugs. They must pay the cost.

It's nowhere near so simple. How do you blame someone who forged his addictions in the pain of being raped repeatedly for years when he still had baby teeth? How can we scold someone for not knowing better when he wasn't raised to be anything else? And where do we place the blame when the victims become aggressors with victims of their own?

I arrange for Darwin to put Keith and me together on a job out of the city. There will be lots of driving, and he'll have no choice but to talk to me. When he shows up to the yard and I tell him this is my plan, he readily agrees.

The job is a condo move from Cochrane to a ranch house further west. It's nearly an hour's drive there, half an hour from load-up to destination, and another hour back to Calgary. I drive the truck, steering with my left hand, holding my voice recorder near Keith with my right. The noise of the engine is formidable, but we're used to talking over it in near-shouts.

The stories pour out of him, incredible ones, terrible ones, tales from his bad years, his life as an addict. At one point he chokes up and needs to pause for several minutes before resuming. I ask him how much of his troubles he traces back to the childhood abuse. "Only my addiction problems," he answers.

"But that's responsible for a lot of the problems in your life, right?"

"Yeah, very much."

"So do you think you would have had a very different life if you hadn't been abused?"

> Yes. I'd have to say yeah. Only because I knew at an early age that my family was fucked in the head. And I tried to separate myself from my family. And I went about it the wrong way. Instead of seeking out someone I could have a chat with and talk to, I masked it all. And I used narcotics to help me mask. And one step led to the next step, led to the next step. And before I knew it, I was an addict. And then I just had no more choice. [...]
>
> I had to feed that monkey that was hanging on my back. [...] I've quit narcotics, three times in my lifespan. And it lasts for a while. I start getting too comfortable, and then thoughts start coming back into my head. And I don't know whether it's my brain tricking me or what. But I think, a little bit of weed here and there, it's gonna be good. But it all boils back to the same thing. That weed starts me off from there, and six months after, weed's no longer good. It doesn't cover it. It doesn't help hide the thoughts in my head. So I go to the next thing. And the worst drug of all that I ever did was crack cocaine. Whether I had bad thoughts in my head of shit that's happened, or not, doesn't matter. I always struggle daily with crack cocaine. It's always there telling me it's okay, I can do this, and I know it's not okay.

I ask Keith what—in a different universe where he was never abused, where he had different opportunities—he would have liked to do with his life.

"It's funny you asked that one. I wanted to be a cop."

"Why?"

"Because I could have helped people."

I press him on his motivation and he explains that he would have made a good cop because of his "upbringing"—that is, his exposure to and association with criminals at a young age.

> Because you're a good people reader. You can judge people, read 'em easier. Not like ... you take a guy who goes to church all his life, he's been a good boy, he was raised a good boy. He isn't a good people reader. He gives everybody the benefit of the doubt. A guy like me, I give zero people the benefit of the doubt. Everybody's out for something in my mind. And that's why I think I would have been a good cop. But I know I could never be one, so I did something else I was good at: moving. And I like to believe I'm really good at my job. I like to believe that's why people like me and let me in.

On our way back into the city, I offer to buy Keith a burger at Boogie's. I steer the truck along Stoney Trail, the freeway bypass that rings Calgary's outer suburbs. It's the long way, but it gives us more time to talk. Keith has never been to Boogie's, and he loves the big, sloppy burger our server puts in front of him. He talks about it for the rest of the week.

I drop Keith off at his home in Inglewood before taking the truck back to the yard. The winter cold cuts through me as I wait at the bus stop, tired muscles shivering as the wind drowns out any remaining sounds of the industrial park at day's end.